DIVING &

Great Barrier Reef

Len Zell

lonely planet

MELBOURNE | LONDON | OAKLAND

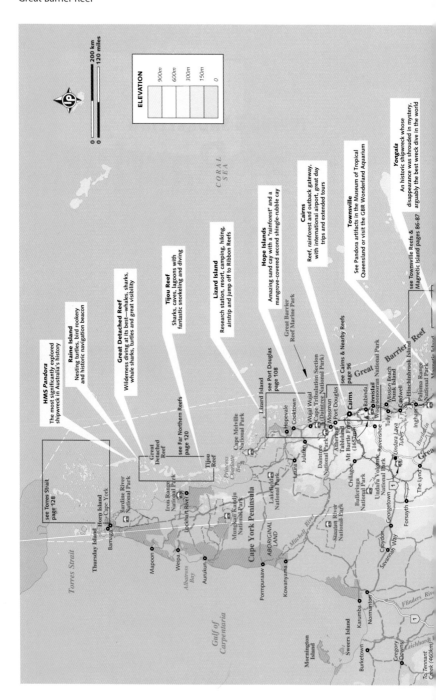

ELEVATION

900m
600m
300m
150m
0

HMS *Pandora*
The most significantly explored shipwreck in Australia's history

Raine Island
Nesting turtles, bird rookery and historic navigation beacon

Great Detached Reef
Wilderness diving at its best—whales, sharks, whale sharks, turtles and great visibility

Tijou Reef
Sharks, caves, lagoons with fantastic snorkeling and diving

Lizard Island
Research station, resort, camping, hiking, airstrip and jump off to Ribbon Reefs

Hope Islands
Amazing sand cay with a "rainforest" and a mangrove-covered second shingle-rubble cay

Cairns
Reef, rainforest and outback gateway, with international airport, great day trips and extended tours

Townsville
See Pandora artifacts in the Museum of Tropical Queensland or visit the GBR Wonderland Aquarium

Yongala
An historic shipwreck whose disappearance was shrouded in mystery, arguably the best wreck dive in the world

see Townsville Reefs & Magnetic Island pages 86–87

CORAL SEA

Great Barrier Reef Marine Park

Lizard Island
see Port Douglas page 108

see Cairns & Nearby Reefs page 96

Palmerston National Park

Great Barrier Reef

Torres Strait

see Torres Strait page 128

Thursday Island
Horn Island
Bamaga
Cape York

Jardine River National Park

Mapoon

Weipa

Iron Range National Park
Lockhart River

Albatross Bay

Aurukun

Mungkan Kaadju National Park

Princess Charlotte Bay

Great Detached Reef

see Far Northern Reefs page 120

Tijou Reef

Cape Melville National Park

Lakefield National Park

Laura

Julatten

Cape Tribulation Section (Daintree National Park)

Daintree National Park

Wujal Wujal
Mossman
Port Douglas

Hopevale

Cooktown

Atherton Tableland

Chillagoe Mt Bartle Frere (1657m)

Bellenden Ker National Park

Undara Volcanic National Park

Ravenshoe

Undara Lava Tubes

Cairns
Babinda
Innisfail

Wooroonooran National Park

Mission Beach
Dunk Island

Tully
Cardwell
Hinchinbrook Island

Ingham
Paluma Range National Park

Magnetic Island

ABORIGINAL LAND

Cape York Peninsula

Mitchell River

Staaten River National Park

Bullseye National Park

Georgetown

Croydon

Savannah Way

Forsayth

The Lynd

Burdekin

Great Barrier Reef

Gulf of Carpentaria

Pompuraaw

Kowanyama

Mornington Island

Sweers Island

Karumba

Normanton

Burketown

Gregory Downs

Flinders River

Leichhardt

To Tennant Creek (460km)

200 km
120 miles

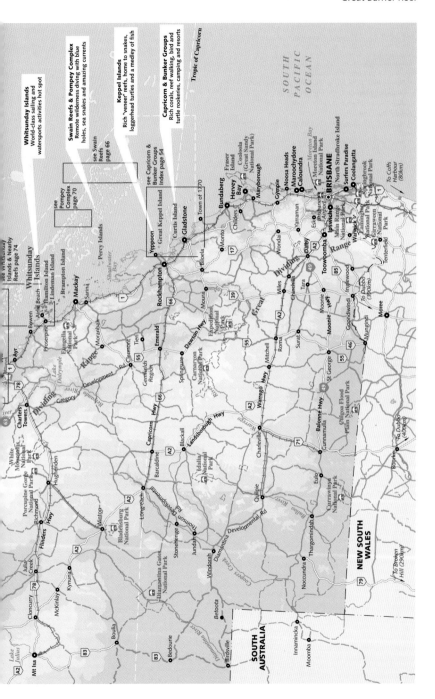

Whitsunday Islands
World-class sailing and watersports activities hot spot

Swain Reefs & Pompey Complex
Remote wilderness diving with blue holes, sea snakes and amazing currents

Keppel Islands
Rich 'veneer' reefs, home to snakes, loggerhead turtles and a medley of fish

Capricorn & Bunker Groups
Rich corals, reef walking, bird and turtle rookeries, camping and resorts

see Swain
Reefs page 66

see
Pompey
Complex,
page 70

see Capricorn &
Bunker Groups
Index page 54

see Whitsunday
Islands & Nearby
Reefs page 74

Whitsunday
Islands

Diving & Snorkeling Great Barrier Reef
2nd edition – September 2006

Published by
Lonely Planet Publications Pty Ltd ABN 36 005 607 983
90 Maribyrnong St, Footscray, Victoria, 3011, Australia
www.lonelyplanet.com

Lonely Planet Offices
Australia Locked Bag 1, Footscray, Victoria, 3011
Phone 03 8379 8000 Fax 03 8379 8111
Email talk2us@lonelyplanet.com.au

USA 150 Linden St, Oakland, CA 94607
Phone 510 893 8555 Toll free 800 275 8555 Fax 510 893 8572
Email info@lonelyplanet.com

UK 72-82 Rosebery Ave London EC1R 4RW
Phone 020 7841 9000 Fax 020 7841 9001
Email go@lonelyplanet.co.uk

Author Len Zell
Publisher Roz Hopkins
Publishing Manager Chris Rennie
Commissioning Editor Ben Handicott
Design Manager Brendan Dempsey
Mapping Development Paul Piaia
Project Management Annelies Mertens
Production Pepper Publishing (Aust) Pty Ltd
Print Production Manager Graham Imeson

Printed by C&C Offset Printing Co Ltd, China
Photographs Len Zell (unless otherwise noted)

ISBN 1740591232

With Many Thanks to
Jennifer Bilos, Jo Vraca, Alison Lyall, Carol Chandler, Amy Carroll, Angus Fleetwood, Tom Calderwood, Sayher Heffernan

Contents

Great Barrier Reef Dive Sites

Imperial Angelfish are extremely shy and rarely seen

Author

LEN ZELL

Len's passion is in the interpretation of coral reefs and the natural environment. As a biologist he has worked on coral reefs for more than 35 years. Len wrote the first edition of this book, Wild Discovery Guides' *A guide to the Kimberley Coast Wilderness* and the soon-to-be-released *Australian Wildlife – Roadkill,* and co-authored Wild Discovery Guides' *Shark Bay-Ningaloo Coast & Outback Pathways WA* with Susie Bedford. Additionally, he has co-written his family history, *Truth Prevails,* edited and published his parent's biographies, *Andy* and *Dulcie* and is presently writing a book on Australian desert tracks with Ian Glover.

Len has been a lecturer and field guide for many expeditionary cruises, private super yachts, luxury cruise lines and outback walks. Two species of coral, *Australogyra zelli* and *Pocillopora zelli,* were named after him for his contributions to marine science.

Len has dived, researched and run educational programs on the Great Barrier Reef, Lord Howe Island, Papua New Guinea, Line Islands, French Polynesia, Cook Islands, Pitcairns, Easter Island, Tonga, Fiji, the Red Sea, Mediterranean and Caribbean. Len has also appeared in documentaries on Channel 9, Discovery Channel, Ushuaia TF1 France, Fox, BBC and many news and current affairs programs.

Len is a skilled lecturer, underwater photographer and adventurer, and was chairman of Dive Queensland for two years and served on the Council of the Australian College for Seniors for two years.

He worked for six seasons on the Queensland Museum's HMS *Pandora* expeditions and was a director of the Pandora Foundation for four years. At the University of Queensland he established AustraLearn, bringing in US students, and TraveLearn, a high quality ecotourism program.

Len has recently returned from an Antarctic expedition and continues to travel around Australia and undertake many expeditionary opportunities.

FROM THE AUTHOR

As well as those who helped so much with the first edition, the author would like to thank the following people for their help and support in gathering information for this book: Nicki Chirlian, Ben Handicott at Lonely Planet, Peter Gesner and the Museum of Tropical Queensland – shipwrecks, Peter Flood for sea-level information and geological details, Gary Barclay, Emily Beresford and Steve O'Malley from Quicksilver Dive and *Silver Sonic* Port Douglas, Heidi Barnes of ProDive Cairns, Julie Ryan of Lizard Island, Alan Irving from Oceania Dive Whitsundays, Judy Burgess of Fantasea Cruises Whitsundays, Liz Davis from Mike Ball Dive Expeditions, Karen Stanaway and John Rumney from *Undersea Explorer,* Sarah Dellar of *Coral Princess,* Peter Gash of Lady Elliot Island, and all those who helped but are too numerous to mention.

The Great Barrier Reef offers thousands
of kilometres of dive site possibilities

Introduction

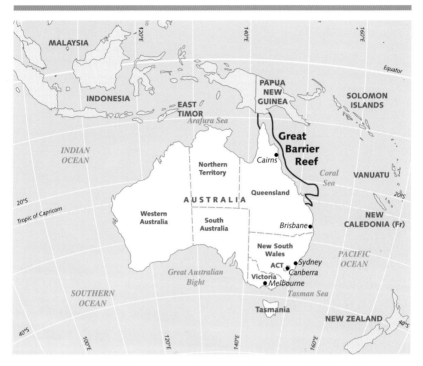

The Great Barrier Reef (GBR) extends along the northeastern Australian coast from Lady Elliot Island in the south, almost to Papau New Guinea in the north. The world's single largest living system, the reef is part of the superb Indo-Pacific coral reef systems, extending from the Red Sea to Easter Island.

Australia, the island continent, is the most desirable tourist destination in the world. Yet many travellers are daunted by the long haul of jet travel it takes to get to this wonderfully unique and friendly country. Those who do make the trip find the effort well worth it. Sophisticated, modern cities and remote country towns lie adjacent to scorching deserts, rolling green and brown pasturelands and winter snowfields. The extremes of climate supports mining, vineyards, crops of all varieties, a profu-

sion of strange wildlife, and a unique human history woven out of the world's oldest human culture, isolation and multiculturalism. All this and some of the best, most accessible diving found anywhere in the world.

Australia has superb diving around its entire coast and in several inland freshwater cave systems, but the big drawcard is the Great Barrier Reef (GBR) – the world's largest and best known reef system. Bigger than Britain, almost the size of Texas (but a lot deeper!) and stretching 2300km (1429 miles) from north to south, the GBR is enormous. This book concentrates on the GBR Province, which encompasses an area of over 1 million sq km (386,109 sq miles), including the whole GBR, nearby Coral Sea reefs (under Australian jurisdiction) and the Torres Strait (under joint

Divers can explore an enormous variety of coral reef habitats

jurisdiction with Papua New Guinea). Most people consider the Great Barrier Reef as being the area that lies within the GBR Marine Park Region (south of 10°41'S at the tip of Cape York Peninsula), whereas the GBR does in fact extend well to the north of here.

Even though the area is lauded as the best protected marine area in the world, it is under severe pressure. Since humans began harvesting marine species, occupying the nearby coast and agriculture about 180 years ago, the near-shore systems have almost totally deteriorated while the mid-shelf and some outer-shelf systems continue to degrade today – some at alarming rates.

Pressures include long-term insidious coastal runoffs, the resuspension of sediments and removal of harvested species and by-catch, through trawling, cyclones, storms, bleaching events, coral growth and crown-of-thorns sea star invasions, which combine with time and the passing of seasons to continually change the appearance of each reef and its surrounds.

The GBR is alive with about 400 species of coral, 2000 types of fish, 4000 molluscs and countless other invertebrates. Six of the world's seven species of sea turtles breed here, and the diversity doesn't stop there. GBR habitats support a myriad of parasitic and single-celled organisms that free-float in the warm tropical waters – between the sand grains, in and on mud flats and sea-grass beds, and among reefs and rocks. All play an important role in the com-

Many people describe the GBR as having the best diving in the world – it has the potential for that title simply because of its size, accessibility, habitat and species diversity. Keep in mind, however, you will not necessarily experience 'brochure weather' – when clear sunny days, calm seas and beautiful people all come together.

To really discover the GBR, you need to be willing to experience it in all weather and seasons. Stick by the old sayings, 'The best diving is in the water' and, 'A bad day's diving is better than a good day's work,' and the GBR will not let you down.

In this guide book, accessible sites are described to enhance your understanding and enjoyment of the GBR's unique ecosystems. In addition, you'll get a brief overview of the primary accessible Coral Sea reefs. For organisational purposes, the dive sites are divided into nine regions and surrounding areas. These include the Capricorn and Bunker Groups (in the south), the Swain Reefs, Pompey Complex, Whitsunday Islands, Townsville and Magnetic Island, Cairns, Port Douglas, Far Northern Reefs and Torres Strait. Several adjacent, regularly dived Coral Sea Reefs also appear in this book.

Some of the sites described are what we refer to as supersites, which give you the choice of diving the whole area or a smaller portion.

Specific information is provided on each dive site. Further details are also included on the behavioural patterns of some of the marine life you can expect to see at various sites, informative notes on reef formations, depth, and recommended diving expertise. There is also some historical insight into some of this area's most famous shipwrecks (the GBR has tortured navigators for centuries!).

When it's time to dry off, turn to the Travel Facts chapter for helpful topside information.

plex food chain and transfer of genetic material throughout the system.

The islands of the GBR range from small, bare sandy 'deserts', often swept away with major storms, to lush rainforest or mangrove masses. Some are home to nesting seabirds and a vast array of wildlife.

Between the reefs and islands are shoal areas of coral and algae (bioherms), with incredible bottom-dwelling animals living on the mud, sand, algal and shell substrates.

With a huge variety of habitats stretching across the continental shelf, the potential for diving, snorkeling and scientific discovery is immeasurable. Those who have dived the GBR thousands of times have only glimpsed the whole system – there are about 3000 reefs!

Facts about Australia

Aussies love the outdoor life

Known as the dry continent, Australia is as big as continental USA and hosts the world's longest surviving human culture. The Aboriginal people arrived more than 50,000 years ago from SE Asia, possibly during a low sea stand during an ice age. It is estimated that the Aboriginal population exceeded one million and was divided into more than 700 clans, each in essence a nation with their own land and dialect of one of around 250 languages. Sadly, much of their cultural and practical knowledge has been lost. James Cook recorded that the Aboriginal people were far happier than he and his fellow English, were well fed and had no 'superfluities' – maybe a message for us today!

The Aboriginal people had many trading networks across the continent and also into SE Asia. They retained information about their travelling routes, food, land boundaries, history, culture, religions, laws and fun in songs. To move through the land of others, they carried message sticks like a passport. This knowledge was occasionally supplemented with paintings in caves and overhangs and many symbols carved into rocks – known as petroglyphs. These works are often referred to as art, though some people believe that term is inappropriate as the works have much deeper meaning than simply 'art.'

The first recorded European discovery of Australia was by Dutch and Portuguese sailors in the 1600s, and New Holland was claimed for the British by James Cook in 1770. It has been suggested by some historians that the Chinese mapped Australia's shores, along with most of the world, in the 1420s. Meanwhile, Macassans had been harvesting and camping on the Australian coast for thousands of years.

Europeans began to arrive in larger numbers from 1788. Since then there have been massive changes. Diseases killed off most of the Aboriginal and Torres Strait Islander populations and those that survived were often shot, poisoned or relocated, which destroyed much of their culture and connection with the land.

Recently, Aboriginal land rights have been exercised, allowing traditional owners access to their traditional lands. Many regard the original concept of Australia as terra nullius (land without owners) as a farce and that the original inhabitants illegally lost their lands.

Many of the early European arrivals until the mid 1800s were convicts and their overseers. A continued influx of immigrants gradually brought new arrivals from all over the world, creating the multicultural mix we see today. As an example, Broome in Western Australia has more than 55 different languages spoken in a town of about 15,000.

In 1901, Australia was declared a Federation of States and the present political system established. Since then a two-party system of adversarial government at the federal, state and local levels has been in operation. The conservative government in power at the time of writing was following closely in the footsteps of the US and Britain.

Agriculture and mining were the first major industries, and fishing, trochus shell, turtle and pearl harvesting were directly associated with the Great Barrier Reef (GBR). Today, tourism and technology have added to the primary industries, but detrimental impact on the environment and atmosphere has continued to increase.

Early Australian settlers razed massive tracts of land, at the cost of the Aboriginal inhabitants, for sheep and later cattle grazing. In the 1930s, the spread of the European rabbit and drought turned much of the country into a dustbowl – a state from which it has yet to recover. The fragile, shallow soils continue to degrade as those with the knowledge of sustainable use desperately try to educate the users of the land and the politicians. These issues of land and water management, coastal run-off effects and overexploitation of natural resources are looming large as massive issues that need to be addressed. Add to these issues the ageing population, and Australia can be seen to be on the cusp of massive changes.

Australia's population is about 20.5 million, mainly concentrated in urban areas (85%) on the coastal fringe, particularly on the coasts of southern Queensland, NSW, Victoria and SW Western Australia. About 25% of the population are first or second generation new settlers with more than 40% of mixed racial origins. The population density of 2.5 persons per square kilometre is one of the world's lowest.

Fast and comfortable day vessels allow divers and snorkelers to experience many offshore and outer edge reef sites.
Photo: www.silverseries.com.au

Fast catamarans run to many reefs for day visitation
Photo: Tourism Queensland

Facts about the Great Barrier Reef & Coral Sea

Pastel reef colours always impress divers and snorkelers
Photo: Andy Lewis

The Great Barrier Reef's waters extend from Lady Elliot Island in the south (offshore from Bundaberg) and north to Bramble Cay and Black Rock in Torres Strait, almost to Papua New Guinea. The GBR should really be named the 'Great Barrier of Reefs' as about 3000 individual reefs – and some 900 islands – are scattered along the Queensland Continental Shelf, with an average water depth of 40m (130ft).

The shelf ranges from as little as 23km (14 miles) wide between Cape Melville and Tydeman Reef, up to 270km (168 miles) wide between Cape Clinton (north of Gladstone and Yeppoon) and Elusive Reef (to the east of the Swain Reefs). This outer edge of the GBR and the continental shelf is fringed by the Queensland Trench, which is up to 2km deep.

East of the Queensland Trench, the flat-topped Coral Sea plateaus give rise to the Coral Sea reefs and atolls. Note that there are atolls in the Coral Sea, but none within GBR waters. About a third of GBR reefs are fringing reefs, dotted along the mainland coast and around most of the mainland type islands. The other two thirds are crescentic, platform, lagoonal or ribbon reefs scattered on the edge of the continental shelf – many with lagoons and/or coral sand bars or cays.

Although the GBR is part of the Coral Sea (which in turn is part of the Pacific Ocean), in this book 'Coral Sea' is used to describe the area of reefs and islands outside the 500m (1640ft) depth contour of the GBR.

Those Coral Sea dive sites that are outside the GBR boundary include a series of atolls and associated islands within Australian territorial waters. Coral Sea reefs covered in this book include Flinders Reefs, Holmes Reef, Bougainville Reef and Osprey Reef, with Bramble Cay in Torres Strait under joint Australian and Papua New Guinean jurisdiction.

The GBR is intimately linked, by the ocean waters and currents, to all other reef systems in the Indian and Pacific oceans. For this reason, most species found in the Red Sea, Hawaii and southeast Pacific have the same or similar species as the GBR. There are few similar species found in the Atlantic Ocean and Caribbean Sea. The centre of diversity of all marine species is in the Sunda Sea in Indonesia and as you move away from there, the number of species diminishes.

Atolls, Cays or Mainland Islands – What's the Difference?

Fairfax Islands and Reef are jewels in the Capricorn Bunkers

Coral Sea Atolls Unlike true coral atolls – ring-like coral islands on reefs that nearly or entirely enclose a lagoon formed on top of a sinking volcano – the outer Coral Sea reefs are a series of reefs surrounding a lagoon on a submerged mountain top or plateau. The inner Coral Sea reefs to the north and south are more like true atolls.

Continental or Mainland Islands These islands are remnants of the mainland, protruding above the sea from the continental shelf. Usually volcanic or sedimentary in origin, they support quite different animals and vegetation than cays. The reefs around these islands are there as a result of the island – the reefs having grown out from the island.

Coral Cays Pronounced both 'kays' and 'keys', cays are there as a result of the reef, formed by debris piled up from the reef tops and edges. This debris is composed mainly of dead coral, shells, calcareous algae and fabulous little single-celled animals called forams. Cays range from pure soft 'coral' sands to those of shingle, rubble and boulders. Some cays, such as Turtle Islands in the north, show remnants of the old fossil reefs from the 2m-higher sea levels of 5000 years ago.

Rainforest, grassy, herbaceous and mangrove plant communities grow on GBR cays, many of which are important bird and turtle nesting areas. Many support vastly different plant communities due to their rainfall and isolation. Green, Heron and Lady Elliot islands are all coral cays, while the mangrove cays at Low and Hope Isles and other reefs to the north, are primarily shingle and rubble, perched on top of coral reefs. Snorkeling in the mangroves is an amazing experience – with corals and shells growing on mangrove roots, horseshoe clams, mini coral heads, seagrasses, upside-down sea-jellies and masses of fish, they're a far cry from the generally held idea of mangroves as muddy, smelly places.

HISTORY

About 18,000 years ago, at the end of the last ice age, sea levels were 130m below present. As the ice melted it caused the sea level to rise at an average of 1.3cm per year. During this time, there would have been periods of rapid rises at a rate faster than walking pace – especially across the flat sections of the shelf. At other times the sea level would have remained stable for extended periods or even fallen. Around 5000 years ago, the sea level was 2m above present levels, then dropped to about the current level, rose again to 1.5m above present, then fell again only to rise 80cm about 1000 years ago.

At least 50,000 years ago, probably during one of the ice-age low sea-stands, the first Australians made their way across land bridges into Australia. Some suggest this occurred in at least three waves. These early inhabitants were likely coastal dwellers who would have initially lived at the edge of today's continental shelf, on areas 130m (420ft) below today's sea surface. As sea levels changed, further migration would have occurred across the submerging coastal plain, away from the old shelf-edge fringing reefs, past the disappearing fossil reefs (which would have resembled flat-topped limestone hills), to the coastal and island situations we see today.

More recent human history suggests the northern areas were used up to 5000 years ago by the Macassan people – a seafaring group with a now traceable genetic presence to the coastal Aboriginal people. Many fishermen from Indonesia today cause problems for Australian Customs and Fisheries as they continue to work these traditional waters.

Gavin Menzies, in his book *1421*, suggests with good evidence that the Chinese had mapped most of the world in the 1420s, and that future explorers had maps from these Chinese expeditions. Certainly Cook recorded in his log that he expected the now-named Endeavour River, where they careened the Endeavour, to be larger.

The first recorded European visit to the (northern) GBR was probably by Portuguese Manoel Gidinho de Eredia in 1601, although there is strong evidence that fellow Portuguese had visited up to 50 years before. A Spaniard, Luis Vaez de Torres, passed through Torres Strait in 1606 but it wasn't until 1770 that Lieutenant James Cook made the first fully recorded 'discovery' of the GBR. Cook had passed through almost two thirds of the complex before he ran aground on it, giving him a good understanding of the problems later navigators would face. He described it as a labyrinth – a term appropriate to this day.

Many others followed. Two outstanding events included William Bligh's long-boat voyage through the area (after the *Bounty* mutiny) in 1789. This voyage produced a quality chart from Bligh Boat Passage and Restoration Island, at Cape Weymouth, to the north. The second event was the wreck of the *Pandora,* which ran aground and sank on the northern GBR in 1791, taking four of the 14 mutineers from the *Bounty* and 31 crew members with her. The *Pandora* wreck, is now well studied and its artefacts are on display in Townsville.

Mainland islands provide many opportunities for visitors to the GBR.
Photo: Tourism Queensland

The *Pandora's* cat was on the topmast the morning after the sinking, but there is no record of it after that.

Matthew Flinders, another great navigator, explorer and scientist, circumnavigated and charted Australia for the British Admiralty during many years. In the early 1800s he charted much of the southern GBR shipping route, its coast and islands, and parts of the Coral Sea. He left the GBR through what is now known as Flinder's Passage. Much of his work was still seen on charts until recently, when satellite imagery and sophisticated side-scan sonar systems replaced the older works.

It wasn't until Lt. Charles Jeffreys, on the brig *Kangaroo,* bravely sailed and charted the inner route in 1815 that more sizable ships were able to take the calmer inside route along the GBR. Jeffreys was followed by fellow navigators Phillip Parker King in the *Mermaid* in 1819 and many others.

Once most of the routes were charted, it was possible for more exploration and, inevitably, exploitation of the area to begin. Beche-de-mer, pearl, turbo and trochus shell harvesting, and guano mining meant many smaller vessels were now plying the waters in addition to passing ships. Scores of ships of all sizes were wrecked during these times and many remain undiscovered.

Much of the older harvesting methods have been improved. Some beche-de-mer fishery continues, and pearl and trochus harvesting still occurs in the north. Today modern vessels sweep large areas of the sea floor and shelf between the reefs, trawling for prawns, scallops, crabs and Moreton Bay Bugs. There has been a major push to reduce this activity due to the destruction of habitat and wasteful by-catch – the discarding of unwanted animals weighing up to 10 times more than the intended catch. An increasing number and variety of small vessels fish for live coral trout, reef fish and the pelagic mackerel and tuna.

By far the greatest use of the reef today is tourism and recreation, with thousands of people visiting the reefs daily.

With the increased use of the nearby coast and the GBR came the need for management. Through the late 1960s and early '70s concerns about limestone mining, oil drilling, general degradation and reef overuse grew. Public concern prompted the establishment of the Great Barrier Reef Marine Park Authority (GBRMPA, known locally as 'ga-broompa') in 1975, set up to manage the waters around the GBR. The Queensland National Parks & Wildlife (QNPW), an offshoot of the Department of Environment, manages the GBR 'lands'. Obviously, the land and water areas overlap, so there is much cooperation between these two organisations, with QNPW undertaking the day-to-day management of the whole GBR Region.

Note: the area within the so-named GBR Marine Park Region is often used to describe the whole GBR, when it in fact leaves out the large area north of 10°41'S – from Cape York to Papua New Guinea. Bear this variance in mind when you see GBR statistics. This book refers to the entire GBR, including the northern Torres Strait section.

Divers, whose personal experiences or baselines of the GBR started around 1970 (as did this author's), have seen it

Pink lace coral is common in GBR overhangs

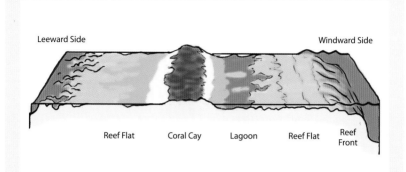

Leeward Side   Windward Side

Reef Flat   Coral Cay   Lagoon   Reef Flat   Reef Front

What is a Coral Reef?

The reefs of the GBR are a thin veneer of living coral, algae and other marine life on top of what could be described as the world's largest rubbish dump. As the corals grow, their symbiotic relationship with the single-celled algae – zooxanthellae – in their tissues produces several waste products. One of these wastes is calcium carbonate, or limestone. As the living layer of corals dump this limestone, each species uses a different stacking design for the crystals. This is what gives us the great and beautiful diversity of hard white coral skeletons.

As the colonies of coral die or are smashed by cyclones or storms, killed by polluted fresh, hot or cold waters, or eaten by parrotfish or crown-of-thorns sea stars, they leave their bleached skeleton behind. These skeletons make ideal settlements for many organisms that cement into the matrix of materials that form a reef. Each reef is thus a jumble of bits and pieces.

Waves and currents are the major factors determining the shape of any reef. Reefs of the GBR tend to have a southeasterly face, which is hammered most of the year by the prevailing southeasterly winds and resultant waves. This leads to the smooth algal rim on the top edge. Spurs, grooves, channels and notches follow the slope down to many different structures determined by depth, location, wave action and currents. Coral and algal structures on the reef fronts tend to be solid and smooth. On the 'back' of the reef we find fragile staghorn coral thickets, shallow plate corals, sand slopes and isolated coral heads (bommies). Occasionally a cyclone or severe storm will bring severe wind and waves from the north or northwest, which can devastate a back-reef edge in a matter of hours. These storms throw large reef colonies onto the reef forming boulder fields.

A reef is like an enormous ocean filter, well described as a 'wall of mouths'. With the high capture rate of nutrients and growth rate of corals and algae, coral reefs are highly productive systems.

The speed in which corals and other reef organisms grow, are smothered, buried, broken or otherwise altered is mind boggling. Different times of day, tide, year, El Niño, La Niña, crown-of-thorns invasions, cyclonic or storm damage, bleaching events or coastal run-off all contribute to this constantly changing world. Just as the coral species and animals determine the shape of the skeleton, the force of the waves and wind determine the shape of the reef and its features overlying the hidden fossil past.

visibly degrade since then. Saying that, it had been subjected to almost 150 years of human impact prior to then, so they were seeing an already severely degraded system. Many argue that the coastal and nearshore systems should never have been included in the declaration of the GBR World Heritage Area as they are so badly degraded. Since the declaration of the GBRMPA there has been a doubling in the insidious coastal runoff effects (faecal matter from grazing animals, fertilizers, pesticides, fungicides and silt from farming and even dog droppings from suburbia!).

Fringing reef corals continue to survive despite heavy sediment loads
Photo: Andy Lewis

On one dive on a mid-shelf reef during the research for this book, the author wrote a note on his slate: 'this reef reminds me of a friend with some insidious cancer – I know they are sick but I don't know what from'. Unfortunately there is insufficient political will to address the issue.

The GBR is only about 500,000 years old. The last series of four ice ages began about 500,000 years ago. After the last ice age – ending about 18,000 years ago – the sea levels rose from 130m below present at an average of about 1.3cm per year for 10,000 years, causing the old fossil reefs to submerge. Sea level reached its present height about 6-8000 years ago, rose 2m 5000 years ago, fell to present level before rising again 1.5m 3000 years ago and fell again before rising 80cm about 1000 years ago. A new veneer of coral grows over the fossil remains of the reefs during each period of submergence and erodes by wind and rain during the dry periods of exposure.

Earlier ideas had the origins of the system from two million years old in the south, and up to 12 million years in the north, due to Australia's slow drift of around 8cm to 10cm per year into the warm tropical waters. Depths of old reef growth vary from 1500m (4921ft) in the Gulf of Papua in the north, 250m (820ft) off Townsville (roughly the middle of the GBR) and 150m (492ft) near Heron Island in the south.

Not a lot of evidence of the ice ages can be 'seen' in the fossil reefs below the latest growth. This lack of evidence is due to erosion that took place while the reefs were dry during the last ice age, when the sea level was 130m (422ft) below its present level. The erosion is evident in layers of land sedimentation over and between the superimposed reef surfaces. Old river beds are still seen in underwater sonar scanning and seismic profiling out to the edge of the continental shelf, between present-day

A dry reef crevasse in 300-million-year-old fossil reef at Windjana Gorge
– Western Australia lets divers walk through what they see underwater

Coral cays are great indicators of geological changes on reefs and important bird nesting and resting sites

reefs. Recent drilling has also found charcoal and mangrove mud below the reefs and underneath the older fossil reefs. Reefs today expose only about a fifth of their total structure – the rest is hidden below the shelf mud, sand and other sediments, washed there during the dry ice ages.

Differing rates of submergence, coastal and tidal affects have caused the great variation in reef structures today. Some are flat-topped platforms of reef. Others are confused masses of little reefs gradually growing together on top of an old submerged reef surface. These are also reflections of the rising or sinking of the coastal edge caused by buckling of the Australian plate.

Archaeologists continue to search for submerged caves on the GBR that may have indications of dry periods and, of greatest excitement, human presence. Caves on Tijou Reef (**Mr Walker's Caves** dive site), may hold some clues to dry periods. Initial research indicates an accumulation rate of about 1m of sediment in the caves for each 1000 years of submergence, with samples cored to 3m so far.

CLIMATE

Weather on the GBR is said, by the locals, to be predictably unpredictable – always expect the unexpected. Being in the southern hemisphere, GBR seasons are the reverse of those in Europe and the US – summer is December to March and winter is June to September.

Because of the length of the GBR, which exists between 9° and 24.5° south (the same distance as New York to Miami, Florida, or the same latitudes and distance as Miami to Trinidad) there is a significant difference in the weather from the north to south. Almost all the GBR complex is in the tropics, except for the reefs south of Heron Island,

Tide Talk

The gravitational pull of the moon and position of the Earth in relation to the sun drive tides so they change throughout the month and year. When the sun and moon are in line, spring tides occur and when at right angles to each other, neap tides occur. Accurate tides tables are available for most of the GBR, but turn to the locals for subtle regional variations. Look for the moon for a fun way to tell approximately where the tide is – a rising moon on the horizon is low tide, mid tide rising is when the moon is at 45°, full tide when directly overhead, mid tide falling at 45° in the west and high tide again at moon set.

Divers like to plan their diving around the neap tides to ensure maximum visibility and lower tide flow. Spring tides bring dirtier water, stronger currents and often worse weather. The GBR generally has tidal changes twice daily – two highs and two lows. At Thursday Island they appear almost random due to the connection, through Torres Strait, between the Coral and Arafura Seas.

At the southern end of the reef and at Townsville, the maximum tide change is about 3m (9ft). As you move toward Broad Sound (between Mackay and Rockhampton), the ranges increase, and usually decrease moving away from the coast. Outside of Broad Sound it is not uncommon to get currents of up to 15km/h (9mph). Local dive operators know

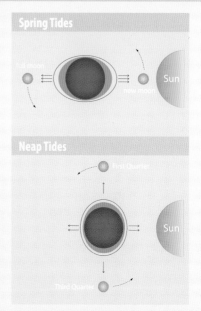

Spring Tides

full moon   Sun   new moon

Neap Tides

First Quarter   Sun   Third Quarter

how to avoid the channels, so don't be concerned – just listen to the briefings.

Drift diving with the tidal currents is a great way to go, but always dive with a 'safety sausage'. Learn how to recognise good safety holds on the bottom, plan your dives, have good surface back-up and you'll be set for some great drift dives. Many divers now dive with a small reef hook, which allows them to hang onto the reef without damage.

Watch aggregations of fish above coral as they will often show breeding behaviour
Photo: Andy Lewis

A branching turret coal filters the passing current for food and light

which straddles the Tropic of Capricorn, so anything below Lady Elliot Island is considered 'sub-tropical'. Distance from the coast and sea-states also influence the weather.

Summer northwest monsoons – seldom extending south of Mackay – give the north a distinct wet season from December to March. It is usually hotter and wetter in the north, with Australia's highest rainfall area on the coast at Tully, just south of Cairns. Humidity during the wet season can be oppressive for short periods, but being on an island or at sea on a boat allows you an escape from the less comfortable weather on the mainland. July to September is drier. Temperatures are cooler in the south – as low as 14°C (57°F) on Lady Elliot Island – and significantly colder on the mainland where there are almost four full seasons.

Winds vary from long periods of calm with occasional medium to strong, but usually gentle, winds – October to February – to cyclonic (hurricane) conditions, which can occur from December to April (a highly effective cyclone warning system is in place in the Pacific). The benefits of diving at this time of the year far outweigh the disadvantages – if there is a cyclone around and you aren't too close, you'll usually have superb calm weather. The prevailing southeasterlies blow from about April to October but can occur any time. Fortunately, most reefs offer a protected side regardless of wind direction.

The water temperature tends to lag behind the air temperature for about one to two months as you go south. The water is warm all year round in the north, from about 24° to 30°C (75° to 86°F). As you head south it gradually gets cooler, dropping to 20° to 28°C (68° to 82°F) in winter.

GBR waters are well mixed so there is usually no distinct thermocline (temperature change) as you go deeper. Thermoclines still occur on hot still days with minimal tide changes or where the colder oceanic waters slop up onto the continental shelf, beneath the warmer shelf waters.

Brochure photographs never reflect the true variability of the GBR's visibility. In coastal areas it is common to have 1m to 3m (3ft to 9ft) visibility, then up to 8m to 15m (26ft to 49ft) just a few kilometres offshore, and 20m to 35m (66ft to 115ft) on the outer edge. In the Coral Sea, 50m (164ft) visibility is common.

Snorkelers delight in GBR opportunities
Photo: LPI

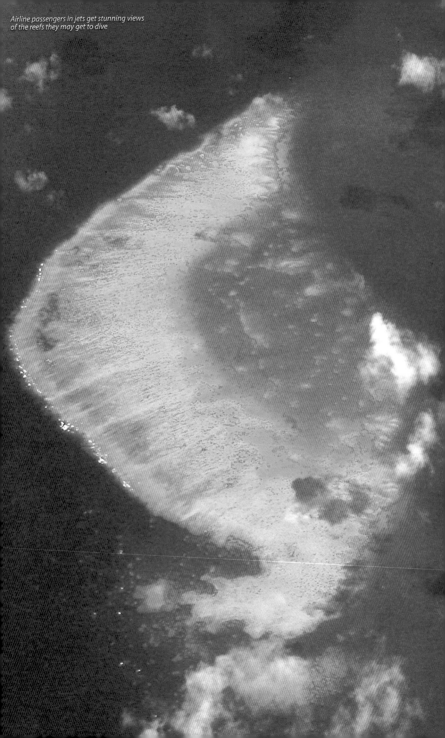
Airline passengers in jets get stunning views of the reefs they may get to dive

Diving the Great Barrier Reef & Coral Sea

Modern vessels provide great diving on the GBR
Photo: www.silverseries.com.au

Even if diving the GBR was your life-long quest, you would only be able see a small part of it. The 3000 reefs and 900 islands – each averaging about 10km (6 miles) of reef edge – means 30,000km (18,642 miles) of possible dive sites. The inter-reefal sea floors and shoals add a further 250,000 sq km (96,527 sq miles) of diveable areas. You'll have an enormous challenge to see even a small part of it.

There are equally exciting diving and snorkeling opportunities in a continuum beyond the GBR. Linked to the GBR, the Coral Sea reefs, islands and shoals offer another enormous area of diving and snorkeling potential. The GBR Province is also connected to nearby reef systems of the Indo-Pacific, which include the eastern Australian coast and Lord Howe Island, from Torres Strait to the Arafura Sea, and the Indian Ocean.

Shipwrecks are the main 'man-made' diving attractions on the GBR and Coral Sea. Queensland has some of the world's best wreck sites – numerous ships have been wrecked on the shallow reefs.

Many remain undiscovered, but those that sank more than 75 years ago are protected by legislation, as are wrecks of decommissioned Royal Australian Navy ships, such as the minesweeper HMAS *Warrnambool*, which was wrecked in 1956 off Cape Grenville.

The GBR lagoon receives half as much water from mainland river run-off as it does from rain. The affect of these fresh water masses on reef life can be dramatic, especially on nearshore and fringing reef systems. Run-off is often loaded with silt, faeces and chemicals from agriculture and other human activities. These freshwater plumes seldom extend beyond 5km (3 miles) from the coast. Inshore winds can re-suspend sediments from the bottom, already stirred up by trawlers or from coastal run-off. These conditions contribute to the low visibility often found around the coastal areas of the Whitsunday Islands, Cairns and Townsville.

As a result, almost all diving and snorkeling in the GBR is boat-based. An exception is Lady Elliot Island, which has a lot of shore dives. Some operations have permanent moorings or pontoons anchored at reef sites, and divers can launch from the pontoons or the boat. You can also charter an amphibious aircraft and fly to several sites for a dive or snorkel. If you camp on one of the islands and have the gear, you can dive right from the beach.

With such a vast number of excellent sites, diving opportunities are almost limitless. This book's coverage is contained to areas that are dived regularly, are accessible by a commercial operator and are part of the GBR Province or Coral Sea.

SNORKELING

All reefs and islands make great snorkeling spots, whether from boats, beaches or headlands. Most snorkeling is done from boats and pontoons anchored on or near reefs.

It's a good idea to cover up to avoid sunburn, especially on the backs of your legs. Also be aware of currents, tides and surf – remember that underwater conditions vary significantly from one region, or even site, to another and with every tide change. Seasonal changes can also alter snorkeling and dive site conditions, influencing the way you dress, what safety and support you require and what techniques you will use.

LIVE-ABOARDS

Most live-aboards run scheduled departure trips to offshore reefs from Bundaberg, 1770, Gladstone, Yeppoon, Mackay, Airlie Beach, Townsville, Cairns, Port Douglas, Cape Tribulation and Cooktown. Trip lengths vary from one to 12 nights. Some go on exploratory trips, others run a set route and may use fixed moorings or pontoons, while

Snorkel, reefs and clear water – absolute paradise

Ribbon reef front and the Coral Sea in the distance

The dive sites in this book are rated according to the following system. These are not absolute ratings but apply to divers at a particular time, diving. For instance, someone unfamiliar with prevailing conditions might be considered a novice diver at one dive area, but an intermediate diver at another location that is more familiar to them.

The 'Depth Range' given for each site refers to the depth the site is usually dived at. A '+' after the maximum depth indicates the site has potential to go much deeper. '0m' depth indicates the reeftop exposes at some low tides but may be 5m underwater at high tides. Some sites have more than one rating, indicating different types of dives are described and available in the area.

Novice

Should be accompanied by a divemaster or instructor on all dives. A novice diver generally fits the following profile:

- basic scuba certification from an internationally recognised certifying agency
- dives infrequently (less than one trip a year)
- logged fewer than 25 total dives
- little or no experience diving in similar waters and conditions
- dives no deeper than 18m (60ft)

Intermediate

An intermediate diver generally fits the following profile:

- may have participated in some form of continuing diver education logged between 25 and 100 dives
- dives no deeper than 40m (130ft)
- has been diving within the last six months in similar waters and conditions

Advanced

An advanced diver generally fits the following profile:

- advanced certification
- has been diving for more than two years and has logged over 100 dives
- has been diving in similar waters and conditions within the last six months

Regardless of skill level, you should be in good physical condition and know your limitations. If you are uncertain as to your own level of expertise, ask the advice of a local dive instructor. He or she is best qualified to assess your abilities based on the prevailing dive conditions at any given site. Ultimately however, you must decide if you are capable of making a particular dive depending on your level of training, recent experience and physical condition, as well as water conditions at the site. Remember that water conditions can change at any time, even during a dive. If an instructor refuses to let you dive at a site, respect their decision – they know the conditions.

Liveaboard vessels provide stunning opportunities for all divers
www.undersea.com.au

others are slightly more impromptu. It is worth checking out various options, as some offer specialist itineraries following marine life events such as minke whales or coral spawning, or offer trips to more remote spots like the far northern reefs, Pompey Complex, Coral Sea Reefs or Swain Reefs.

Some operators will transport you out to a vessel permanently moored at an ideal site, which you can then explore at your leisure during an extended period.

Great Barrier Reef vessels are available for charters of varying lengths. Many dive charter vessels have roaming permits that allow them to operate in most of the GBR Region and the Coral Sea.

Some operators also have annual scheduled trips to a special, remote area of reefs, so it is worth contacting them to find out what trips they have planned. Also, operators may have spaces on someone else's charter, which you may be able to slot into, although this is less common and unreliable.

The listing of live-aboard operators recommended in this book includes only Dive Queensland members, who follow a set of agreed standards. For the latest membership list, visit www.dive-queensland.com.au. Ideally, operators should also be highly accredited by the Ecotourism Association of Australia.

Several other vessels offer cruises that include diving, but it's not their primary focus. These include cruises from Townsville to Cairns or from Cairns to Lizard Island, which view good snorkeling and diving as adjuncts to good cruising.

CERTIFICATION

All Queensland diver training facilities are aligned with one of the internationally recognised diver training agencies. Most operators do a good job – it's just that many do a better job. Things change with new ownership, experience of operation and staff, so research well before deciding. If you can, ask recent students and clients about their experience, and find out as much as you can about the operation itself.

This book only recommends members of Dive Queensland. They meet the association standards and offer instruction, from introductory courses to advanced training and other specialty courses. Charter vessels may have a Divemaster on board or be able to supply instructors on request for an extra fee.

The GBR is a great place to learn to dive, but be aware that most diving you will do after this will not compare! It may be better to learn elsewhere and then spend the time here enjoying your skill and the reef life.

Best Wreck Dive

Yongala: an oasis in the sandy desert sea floor with stunning marine life.

Best Shark Dive

Osprey Reef North Horn: grey reefs, silvertips, whitetip reef and hammerhead sharks, often close-up.

Best Drift Dive

On a rising tide at Bligh's Boat Entrance or any of the channels in between the Ribbon Reefs or down in the Pompey Hard-Lines. Vertical walls, big animals, great small animals.

Best Critter or Muck Dive

Watson's Bay: Lizard Island out in 17m of water with solitary corals, amazing tozeumid shrimp, worms, sea cucumbers with commensal shrimps.

Best Cave Dive

Mr Walker's Caves: situated on Tijou Reef, these caves are instructive in marine life, sea level changes and possibly human history. There is incredible life, but it can be a bit scary at times.

Best Reef Dive

The Great Barrier! Great Detached Reef off the front, and for those who can't get there, the fronts off Cairns and Port Douglas, or Just Magic off the Whitsundays.

Best Blow Hole

The Blow Hole at Lady Elliot Island and those similar on many other GBR reefs. Wave-worn holes formed during lower sea stands now inhabited by amazing life.

Best Fish Dive

The Heron Island Bommie with masses of emperor, wrasse, coral trout, little fish, moray eels, cleaner wrasse – take plenty of data storage!

Best Big Fish Dive

The Cod Hole on Ribbon Reef No. 10. Truly a world class experience.

ACTIVITIES & ATTRACTIONS

Queensland, the 'Sunshine State' has an almost endless variety of land and water-based tourism opportunities. Rainforest excursions and outback activities abound and excellent accredited ecotourism operators provide numerous opportunities right along the coast.

The enormous range of habitats on the GBR – its islands, coast and nearby Coral Sea – offer almost every conceivable watersport and land activity in addition to diving and snorkeling.

Underwater for non-divers

Several operators out of Cairns are using systems that allow non-divers to 'dive' using surface-supplied air systems. Both use a surface supplied helmet and on one you ride an underwater scooter through the water like a motorcycle, while with the other you walk on the bottom. These are highly controlled and restrictive compared to diving due to the needs for protecting the participant. That said, they are great fun and provide an outstanding way for non-divers to experience the world with an ease and enjoyment that most divers take for granted.

Island Camping

Pitching a tent on an island is a unique and affordable way to experience the GBR. Camp site facilities range from virtually nothing to showers, interpretive signage, self-composting toilets, flush toilets and picnic tables. Most of the islands are national parks and permits from the EPA are required before you can land on them.

All the islands have fragile ecosystems so introduced insects and seeds can have devastating impacts. Camp only in the designated areas, keep to all marked tracks and take out all you brought in, including the garbage. Fires are banned

Snorkelers enjoy a bommie under the watchful eye of their boatman
Photo: www.coralprincess.com.au

so you need a gas stove or similar. Most islands are remote so ensure you follow the EPA advice in regard to medical and general emergencies. Lists of what you need to bring can be obtained from the EPA and some operators. Weather can often prevent planned pickups, so plan for an extra week or so of stay with ample water and food.

Hiking & Island Walking

There are hiking trails to explore on the Whitsunday Islands, Hinchinbrook Island and Lizard Island, and plenty of opportunities for 'island walks' on the smaller islands. Each island provides an excellent viewing of wildlife and vegetation. Some islands are often closed to visitors to protect breeding wildlife.

The cays of Swain Reefs, Capricorn Bunkers, Bushy Island south of the Whitsundays, and the far northern areas are excellent, with vegetation differences due to rainfall, seeds dropped from feeding pigeons, or the coral shingle or rubble substrate of the cay. Some rubble cays have mangrove stands, such as Nymph, Hope, Two, Three, Howicks, the Low Isles, Turtle Islands, and others to the north almost to Papua New Guinea.

Crocodiles have been recorded on several of the far northern islands up to 100km (62 miles) off the coast, so keep your eyes open for tracks.

Mainland or continental islands – including the Whitsundays, Percys, Keppel, Palm, Family, Frankland, Sir Charles Hardy, Forbes, Albany Groups and those of the Torres Strait – carry unique vegetation, human history and excellent beaches.

When visiting any island, stay well away from nesting birds, turtles or other wildlife. Human intervention can create major disturbances to some species. Also, check that you haven't got any seeds in your socks, clothes or shoes before stepping onto an island. Always carry plenty of water and be sun-safe.

Whale Watching

Whale watching is an activity that leaves people emotionally changed and charged. Several species of whales can be seen on the GBR, especially humpback and minke whales. Sperm and Bryde's whales are less common. The smaller whales – dolphins, porpoises, killer and pilot whales – are much more common, although dolphins are rarely seen underwater.

Laws govern the approach and interaction with whales – basically let the whales come to you and then let them determine the interaction. Minkes are commonly seen off off the coast between Cairns and Lizard Island in June/July, and humpbacks appear from the southern GBR to Townsville from May to October. Snorkeling with the minkes is a wonderful experience, when it occurs. Humpbacks can only be observed from a boat unless you're lucky enough to have the rare experience of an underwater encounter, where the whale comes to you.

Reef Walking

Many reefs of the southern GBR are regularly exposed at low tide, while other parts are exposed during extreme tides, allowing visitors to walk on the reeftop. Reef walking is a fantastic way to learn about marine life, and view organisms from another perspective, especially if accompanied by a naturalist who can identify organisms and their behavioral patterns.

Humpback whales are easily recognised by their enormous pectoral fins.

Walking on the Reef

Reefwalking is a stunning experience for all.

You may ask: Doesn't walking on coral kill it? In some cases – yes. A reeftop is a combination of living and apparently 'dead' surfaces. In actual fact, the dead areas are usually rich algal turfs full of small creatures like shrimps, copepods, amphipods and worms. The sandy areas have many animals living between the grains, and the living coral is easy to see. These areas are extremely robust and quite safe to explore with a guide – without a guide it is important to walk in the areas designated by Marine Parks, as some areas are much more fragile than others.

For an enjoyable and successful reef walk, follow these few hints:

· plan your walk
· check tide times so you don't get caught out; follow the tide out and return as soon as it begins to rise again
· tell someone where you are going
· check local rules
· wear a hat, long sleeve shirt, strong shoes and socks to protect ankles from coral cuts
· do not touch any animal unless the guide hands it to you
· use maximum protection sunscreen but be sure not to get it on the animals
· try using a mask or viewing device to see into the deeper water
· put your camera on a short strap so that when you bend over you don't dunk it
· bring plenty of film or data storage and batteries
· remember, every surface of the reef has life growing on or in it:
· watch where you put your feet
· walk in sandy tracks between living coral
· avoid walking near edges of pools as the coral is fragile and can collapse
· if you turn over a boulder, carefully ensure it goes back the way it was
· leave reef life where it is – remember, even touching many reef organisms can kill them.

Can you believe he got champagne,
cheese and crackers after this photo?

Camping on islands is a special exposure to this amazing reef and island system

Manta Towing

No, you will not be riding manta rays! 'Manta towing' is simply a term used for one of the fastest and most exciting ways to see a lot of reef. It was developed by researchers for rapid reef surveys. It's a marine-ply board that's 60cm (24 inches) by 30cm (12 inches), attached to a rope bridle on the middle of each side with a hand hold in the middle at the back and linked by 30m (100ft) of tow rope to a dinghy.

The boat driver (with an observer on board) keeps as close as safely possible to the reef edge while pulling you along in your snorkeling gear. You tilt the board to glide through the ocean (it takes several attempts before you get the hang of it).

A hand waved up and down tells the driver to slow down, and a spinning finger means speed up. Some people just

Camping is available on the following islands. See **http://www.epa.qld.gov.au/parks_and_forests/find_a_park_or_forest/** or visit the appropriate environmental office for permits and information.

Island	Office location
Capricorn Group	Gladstone
Keppel Group	Rockhampton
Cumberland Group	Mackay
Whitsunday Islands	Whitsunday
Orpheus Island	Cardwell
Hinchinbrook Island	Cardwell
Family Islands	Cardwell
Dunk Island	Cardwell
Lizard Island Group	Cairns
Turtle Islands	Cairns
Flinders Group	Cairns
Three Isles	Cairns

hang onto a rope and get towed along, which is good, but not as fun as the underwater acrobatics – spirals, barrel rolls and porpoising – you can achieve on a manta board.

Manta towing is used by researchers for community surveys, crown-of-thorns seastar counts and by divers to find the best sites. Never use scuba gear while getting towed, as this can quickly lead to embolisms.

Semi-Submersibles

Most reef operations today offer semi-submersibles (or 'semi-subs'). These powered boats have large glass windows below the surface and offer extremely safe reef viewing. You look through clear or plankton-rich waters and float by stunning coral, fish, turtles, rays and sharks – all without getting wet! Trips can be a little nauseating in

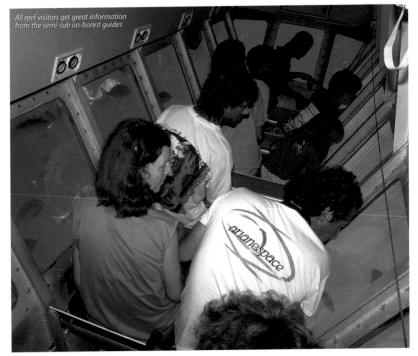

All reef visitors get great information from the semi-sub on-board guides

rough conditions, but the water is usually calm behind reefs and islands. This is an excellent way for non-divers to get a glimpse of what divers experience and benefit from a guide's comprehensive commentary about the reef life.

Windsurfing

Windsurfing is a popular activity throughout the GBR. Gear can be rented at mainland and island resorts, while some charter and dive boats carry their own.

Caution should be observed as many inexperienced people get so far downwind from their boats or islands that they can't get back. Make sure someone is watching out for you in case you get into trouble – a kilometre (.6 mile) at sea is a long way to paddle a windsurfer against wind and chop. It is important to have good sun protection, and wear sunglasses well fixed to your

Beware the s!

The world's largest estuarine predator reminds us to be careful near the water's edge on the mainland and nearshore islands in the north

Estuarine crocodiles, or 'salties', occur in inland rivers, creeks and estuaries along Queensland's coast and occasionally on islands 100km (62 miles) out to sea.

National Park signs indicate locations that pose a risk of a crocodile encounter.

If you find yourself in crocodile territory, avoid repetitive behaviour and avoid, or be very careful near, the water's edge. Although it's the unseen crocodiles that are a problem, don't let the threat of them keep you indoors or away from reef waters. There has only been one record of a diver being bitten by an estuarine crocodile – a research diver undertaking a survey on an inshore reef rarely visited by recreational divers.

A second species, the smaller Freshwater Crocodile, occurs in inland freshwater systems, but is not considered as dangerous.

Learning About the Reef

As divers discover more they slow down and discover even more

Many varieties of interpretive reef services exist on the GBR mainland, islands and boats. Members of the Ecotourism Association of Australia only use accredited guides.

Reef Biosearch (www.quicksilver-cruises.com/marine_ecology_information.php) was the first real marine ecotourism operation and has maintained a long-term quality reputation as an educational, interpretive and research operation. It provides excellent on-board marine biologists for Quicksilver Cruises (www.quicksilver-cruises.com/reef_trips.php) and their subsidiary operations, and also undertakes research and advisory roles in cooperation with reef management and research agencies.

An excellent way to learn about coral reef and fish growth, reproduction, identification and threats, is Reef Teach (☎ (07) 4031 7794; www.reefteach.com.au/Great_Barrier_Reef. htm; 14 Spence Street, Cairns). It offers slide shows, films and lectures given by well qualified marine biologists, and also tips on underwater photography, diving and snorkeling on the GBR. Accreditation is available for some courses. This is an advisable program to do before you go diving.

In the water, the Undersea Explorer (☎ (07) 4099 5911; info@undersea.com.au; www. undersea.com.au) leads the way by positively linking tourism with scientific research. This live-aboard conducts its main research from Port Douglas to the Ribbon Reefs and to Osprey Reef in the Coral Sea. In addition to a unique diving experience you'll get to take part in valuable research while learning more about the reefs. It takes recreational divers on research expeditions to learn more about minke whales, turtles, sharks, nautilus and other reef life. Many operators take along a marine biologist or naturalist on all dive trips, to enhance divers' understanding and appreciation of the reefs.

Based on Magnetic Island is Reef EcoTours, one of several operations that provide ecotourism and coral reef ecology training for student groups at all levels and locations as well as consultancy services.

AustraLearn out of Denver is an operation that allows US students to study abroad in Australia within the university system.

head. Gloves and dive booties will help prevent abrasions and allow for better control of the board.

Parasailing

Parasailing is available at some resorts and mainland centres. It is a great way to get a low aerial perspective of the nearby features and a great buzz at the same time. The ride out in the speed boat, the rigging up and the lift off into the sky are gentle and easy. Bring your camera and get some unrepeatable shots – just make sure your camera is splash-proof and fixed on well. Safety standards are high and the laws require equipment to be well-maintained.

Joy Flights

Joy flights in helicopters and light aircraft are available from most major centres and resorts. This is a fabulous way to get some great pictures and understanding of the reef shapes, sizes and relationships with each other and nearby islands or the mainland. Fly between 9am and 3pm using a polarizing filter on your camera and polarizing sunglasses for the best views. Beware of the polarizing effect through some perspex windows – you may find you have to remove the filter, or the window!

Sailing

Cruising – bareboat or crewed – is superb around the Whitsunday Islands (possibly the best in the world) and in some areas around Hinchinbrook Island. You can rent yachts of all sizes and powered vessels at many mainland and offshore resorts. Tourist information centres can assist in planning for rentals in advance.

Dive operators and some charter planes will pick guests up from their vessel for day dive trips on request. Snorkeling is very good all around the Whitsundays and many great swimming beaches are available. An excellent book, *100 Magic Miles of the Reef – The Whitsunday Islands by David Colefelt*, is an excellent detailed guide to the area with great charts, dive sites, fishing information, resorts, aerial photos and navigational hints.

Lady Musgrave Island and reef is a fantastic diving, day visitor and camping site

Diving Conservation & Awareness

Male loggerhead turtles are often found at the reef backs of the Capricorn Bunkers. Be careful as they have been known to try to mate with divers

MARINE RESERVES & REGULATIONS

The GBR Region is a World Heritage Area and the world's largest marine park, giving Australia more reefs under its control than any other country. The areas of the GBR outside the GBRMP are in the jurisdiction of the state of Queensland or the Australian Nature Conservation Agency (Coral Sea Territories), while Torres Strait is under joint management of Australia and Papua New Guinea. Areas above low-water are in Queensland's jurisdiction and they and the GBRMP are managed by Queensland's Environmental Protection Agency (EPA).

The Marine Park is a multi-use zoning system ranging from no-access areas to national parks. The whole area is protected from littering, spearfishing using scuba, oil drilling and mining. Less than 1% of the Great Barrier Reef is closed to recreational diving but on the entire GBR, your diving practice should follow the 'look, don't touch' system.

Queensland National Parks & Wildlife (QNPW) handles the on-site (land) management of the GBR national parks. Rules for conduct within these areas can be found at a Marine Parks office or the GBRMPA website (www.gbrmpa.gov.au), which has zoning maps for each area.

GOVERNMENT ORGANISATIONS

**Great Barrier Reef Marine
Park Authority (GBRMPA)**
PO Box 1379
Townsville, QLD 4810
☎ (07) 4750 0700
www.gbrmpa.gov.au

**Queensland Environmental
Protection Agency (EPA)**
Bushfires, medical and other
emergencies: ☎ 000
EPA Hotline
(Inquiries – 24 hrs): ☎ 1300 130 372

Campsite bookings:
☎ 13 13 04; www.qld.gov.au/camping

Ecoaccess Customer Service Unit:
☎ 1300 368 326 (For information
about environmental and wildlife
licences and permits)

Head Office – Brisbane
EPA Customer Service Centre
160 Ann Street,
Brisbane, QLD 4000
Open: 8.30am-5.00pm Mon-Fri
PO Box 15155
City East, QLD 4002
☎ (07) 3227 8185
www.epa.qld.gov.au

Dive groups camp on many GBR islands

REGIONAL QUEENSLAND PARKS & WILDLIFE SERVICE OFFICES

Central
Rockhampton Regional Office
61 Yeppoon Road,
North Rockhampton, QLD 4701
☎ (07) 4936 0511
Gladstone: ☎ (07) 4971 6500
Mackay: ☎ (07) 4982 4555
Rosslyn Bay: ☎ (07) 4933 6595
Whitsunday: ☎ (07) 4946 7022

Northern
Old Quarantine Station,
Cape Pallarenda Road
Townsville, QLD 4810
☎ (07) 4722 5211

Cairns Regional Office
☎ (07) 4046 6600

Cardwell
☎ (07) 4066 8601

**Queensland Department of Primary
Industries and Fisheries**
Primary Industries Building
80 Ann St,
Brisbane, QLD
GPO Box 46,
Brisbane, QLD 4001
☎ 13 25 23 or
☎ (07) 3404 6999
Open 8.00am to 8.00pm daily.
This department is responsible for
protecting and conserving fisheries
resources while maintaining profitable
commercial and enjoyable recreational
fishing sectors.

**Environment Australia
Biodiversity Group**
PO Box 636
Canberra, ACT 2601
☎ (02) 6250 0200
This group is responsible for manage-
ment of the Coringa, Herald and Lihou
National Nature Reserves in the Coral
Sea.

RESPONSIBLE DIVING

Dive sites are generally located where the reefs and walls display the most beautiful corals and sponges. It only takes a moment – an inadvertently placed hand or knee on the coral or an unaware brush or kick with a fin – to destroy this fragile and delicate living ecosystem.

Please consider the following tips when diving and help preserve the ecology and beauty of the reefs:

- Maintain proper buoyancy control and avoid over-weighting. Be aware that buoyancy can change over the period of an extended trip: initially you may breathe harder and need more weighting; a few days later you may breath more easily and need less weight.
- Use the correct weight belt position to stay horizontal (ie. raise the belt above your waist to elevate your feet/fins, and move it lower toward your hips to lower them).
- Use your tank position in the backpack as a balance weight (ie. raise your backpack on the tank to lower your legs, and lower the backpack on the tank to raise your legs).
- Be careful about buoyancy loss at depth; the deeper you go the more your wetsuit compresses, and the more buoyancy you lose.
- Photographers must be extra careful. Cameras and equipment affect buoyancy. Changing f-stops, framing a subject, and maintaining position for a photo often conspire to prohibit the ideal 'no-touch' approach on a reef. So, when you must use 'holdfasts,' choose them intelligently (ie. use one finger only for leverage off an area of dead coral).
- Avoid full leg kicks when working close to the bottom and when leaving a photo scene. When you inadvertently kick something, stop kicking straight away! Seems obvious, but some divers either semi-panic or are totally oblivious when they bump something. When treading water in shallow reef areas, take care not to kick up clouds of sand. Settling sand can easily smother delicate reef organisms.
- When swimming in strong currents, be extra careful about leg kicks and handholds.
- Attach dangling gauges, computer consoles, and octopus regulators securely. They are like miniature wrecking balls to a reef.
- Never drop boat anchors onto a coral reef, and take care not to ground boats on coral. Encourage dive operators and regulatory bodies to establish permanent moorings at popular dive sites.
- Resist the temptation to collect or buy corals or shells. Aside from the ecological damage, taking home marine souvenirs depletes the beauty of a site and spoils the enjoyment of others.
- Resist the temptation to feed fish. You may disturb their normal eating habits, encourage aggressive behaviour, or feed them food that is detrimental to their health.

Class is in – these divers begin their greater underwater discovery

MARINE ENVIRONMENTAL ORGANISATIONS

Australian Organisations

There are numerous government, NGOs and voluntary organisations with direct interests in the GBR. When the GBRMPA called a strategic planning workshop, more than 75 of these organizations with direct interests were invited. Some are shown below.

Australian Conservation Foundation

Head Office
Floor 1, 60 Leicester St,
Carlton, Victoria 3053
☎ 1800 332 510 (free call) or
☎ (03) 9345 1111
www.acfonline.org.au

Cairns
Suite 1/Level 1, 96– 98 Lake Street,
Cairns, QLD 4870
☎ (07) 4031 5760
Australia's central conservation organisation, with considerable efforts directed towards the GBR and Coral Sea.

Australian Coral Reef Society (ACRS)

c/- Centre for Marine Studies
Level 7, Gerhmann Building
The University of Queensland
St Lucia QLD 4072
☎ (07) 3365 4333
www.australiancoralreefsociety.org
The ACRS promotes scientific research on Australian coral reefs and is a forum for discussion and information transfer among scientists, management agencies and reef-based industries that are committed to ecological sustainability.

Australian Institute of Marine Science (AIMS)

PMB 3, Townsville MC
Townsville, QLD 4810
☎ (07) 4753 4444
www.aims.gov.au
An Australian Commonwealth Government agency established in 1972 to educate, sustain and protect the marine environment through scientific research.

Australian Marine Conservation Society (AMCS)

PO Box 5136
Manly, QLD 4179
☎ 1800 066 299 (freecall) or
☎ (07) 3393 5811
www.amcs.org.au
This national, not-for-profit charity protects the health and vitality of Australia's coasts and oceans. It is a consistent and persuasive voice on a wide range of marine issues throughout Australia, including the declaration of marine protected areas, sustainable fisheries, recovery of threatened species and land-based pollution.

Low Isles Preservation Society (LIPS)

PO Box 104
Port Douglas, QLD 4871
www.lips.org.au
This conservation group is dedicated to the protection and preservation of the Low Isles, the marine, coastal and rainforest environments of far north Queensland.

Order of Underwater Coral Heroes (OUCH)

PO Box 180
Airlie Beach, QLD 4802
☎ (07) 4946-7435
www.ouchvolunteers.org
A non-profit organisation made up of volunteer members from Australia and abroad who donate their time and effort to protecting the reefs.

Seagrass-Watch HQ

Northern Fisheries Centre
PO Box 5396 Cairns, QLD 4870
☎ (07) 40 350 100
www.seagrasswatch.org.au
A community-based monitoring program raising awareness on the condition of nearshore seagrass ecosystems.

Responsible divers have minimal or no impact on reef life

International Organisations

The following international groups are actively involved in promoting responsible diving practices, publicising environmental marine threats, and lobbying for better policies.

The Coral Reef Alliance (CORAL)

417 Montgomery Street,
Suite 205
San Francisco, CA 94104, USA
☎ 1-888-CORAL-REEF (toll free) or
☎ 415-834-0900
www.coral.org
This member-supported, non-profit organisation is dedicated to keeping coral reefs alive by integrating ecosystem management, sustainable tourism and community partnerships.

Coral Forest

201 William Street
Key West , FL 33041, USA
☎ 305-294-3100 (USA)
A non-profit, environmental organisation that aims to protecting coral reef ecosystems through education as well as action.

Reef Check

www.reefcheck.org
A volunteer-based, ocean conservation organisation that aims to save coral reefs globally.

Cousteau Society

☎ 757-523-9335 (USA)
www.cousteau.org/en
Educating people to understand and protect water systems for the well-being of future generations.

Project AWARE Foundation

☎ 714-540-0251 (USA)
www.projectaware.org
A diving industry voluntary organisation established to educate, advocate and act to conserve the marine environment.

ReefKeeper International

An advocacy organisation established to protect coral reefs and their marine life.
☎ 305-358-4600 (USA)
www.reefkeeper.org

Collecting Reef Items

Collecting any item – alive or dead – in the GBR Marine Park is an offence if you don't have a permit. If you want to collect anything, check with your local Marine Parks office to obtain the relevant permit, which will have various restrictions and reporting requirements. Giant clams, turtles, baler and helmet shells are fully protected. It is illegal to export any shells, turtle or coral products from Australia.

The annual coral reef orgasm of breeding is a
spectacular upside-down underwater snowstorm

Diving Health & Safety

GENERAL OVERVIEW

Australia is a remarkably healthy country, considering so much of it is in the tropics. The hot sun often leads to heat exhaustion, sunstroke or severe sunburn for those who don't take care. Always wear a hat, strong sunscreen and a shirt, and drink plenty of water. Sunglasses, especially those with polarised lenses are ideal. When snorkeling always ensure the backs of your legs are protected – a full body lycra suit is best.

There are numerous tropical diseases found in Queensland, especially the north. Ross River Fever, Dengue Fever, Japanese Encephalitis and Barmah Forest virus are some of the better known. All can be avoided by ensuring you don't get bitten by mosquitoes.

While Queensland has the safest diving record in the world and regulations are continually updated to maintain this standard, you need to be aware and prepared for your own diving safety.

PRE-TRIP PREPARATION

Your personal fitness is important as there can be strong currents, waves and surges, as well as the opportunity for multiple dives. Your general state of health, diving skill level and specific equipment needs are the three most important factors on any dive trip. If you honestly assess these before you leave – even before selecting your dive destination – you'll be well on your way to ensuring a successful, safe dive trip.

Feeling good physically, diving with experience and with reliable equipment will not only increase your safety, but will also enhance your enjoyment underwater. If you're not in shape, start exercising. If you haven't dived for a while (six months is too long) and your skills are rusty, make a local dive with an experienced buddy or take a scuba review course. Inspect your dive gear.

Pre-trip planning is always wise, but for a scuba trip, it's critical. Be careful not

Relaxed divers can spend more time watching reef life

to 'get in over your head,' so to speak. Standards vary among countries and among dive operations. If you have little diving experience, it would be wise to select a popular resort area or boat that sees a lot of new divers, has modern medical facilities and provides reliable rental gear. On the other hand, if you're in good shape, dive a lot and have your own gear, you might choose a more remote area or operator that requires greater self-reliance. If your skills aren't up to scratch then discuss the situation immediately with the local divemaster so they can plan a way of helping you without detracting from the diving of the other guests.

At least a month before you leave, inspect your dive gear. Remember, your regulator should be serviced annually, whether you've used it or not. If you use a dive computer, check the battery level. If it's low and you can replace the battery yourself, change it before the trip or buy a spare one to take along. Otherwise, send the computer to the manufacturer for a battery replacement.

If possible, find out if the dive centre rents, or can service, the type of gear you own. If not, you might want to take spare parts or even spare gear. Bringing along a spare mask is always a good idea as well.

Purchase any additional equipment you might need, such as a dive light and tank marker light for night diving, a line reel for wreck diving, etc. Make sure you have at least a whistle attached to your BC and alternate air source, as these are required by law in Queensland. Add a marker tube (also known as a safety sausage or come-to-me).

About a week before taking off, do a final check of your certification card and gear, grease o-rings and check batteries. Don't forget to pack personal medications such as decongestants, ear drops, antihistamines and seasickness tablets. To enter Australia you need no immunisations, but it's best if you fill your own prescriptions before departure as drugs vary.

BEFORE YOU SNORKEL

Snorkeling is generally a safe activity, however it does require some physical exertion.

Take special precautions and inform the divemaster if you suffer from any of the following conditions: heart disease, high or low blood pressure, shortness of breath (especially when exercising), asthma, emphysema, any other chronic lung disease, epilepsy, fits or faints, recent head injury or concussion, and diabetes (especially if needing medical attention). It is not advisable to snorkel after any alcohol consumption.

Diving & Flying

Most divers to the GBR arrive by air. While it's fine to dive soon after flying, it's important to remember that your last dive should be completed at least 12 hours (most advise 24 hours) before your flight, even in a balloon or for a parachute jump, in order to minimise the risk of residual nitrogen in the blood that can cause decompression injury.

TIPS FOR EVALUATING A QUEENSLAND DIVE OPERATOR

First impressions mean a lot. Does the business appear organised and professionally staffed? Does it prominently display a membership of Dive Queensland, Queensland Charter Vessel Association and a dive affiliation such as NAUI, PADI, SSI? Does it show accreditation from the Ecotourism Association of Australia? These are good indications that the operation adheres to high standards. There are still a few 'cowboy' operations out there – don't let them turn you into another diving injury statistic!

Before taking you diving, a well-run business will always have paperwork for you to fill out, will treat you well and show you around. At the least, they should look at your certification card and ask when you last dived. If the operator wants to see your logbook or check basic skills in the water, that is even better.

Rental equipment should be well-rinsed and stored. If you see sand or salt crystals, watch out – go somewhere else. Before starting on your dive, inspect the equipment thoroughly: check the hoses for wear, ensure mouthpieces are secure and make sure there is a depth gauge, air pressure gauge, computer and octopus, as required by law in Queensland.

After gearing up and turning on your air, listen for air leaks. Now test your BC: push the power inflator to make sure it functions correctly (and doesn't free-flow); make sure the BC holds air and the auto-overpressure valve functions well; if it fails, get another BC – don't try to inflate it manually. Then purge your regulator a bit and smell the air. It should be odourless. If you detect an oily or otherwise bad odour, try a different tank, or maybe it would be better to start searching for another operator. Equipment and breathing air must pass regular inspections and Australian Standards.

Snorkelers get close up and personal with giant clams

MEDICAL FACILITIES

Coastal centres have excellent medical support, with most resorts having a nurse and nurse station on site. Boats are equipped with a medical kit, which the crew can use under instruction from a mainland doctor via radio or telephone. All dive vessels are required by law to have oxygen systems and supplies on board, as well as staff trained in their use. It helps if you ask to see the systems and supplies and know how they work.

For non-diving sickness or injury, your operator will direct you to the best local medical facilities. Each major city has a central hospital and 24-hour medical clinics. Pharmacies are always useful for advice about minor problems not requiring prescription drugs.

DIVING EMERGENCIES

If in the unfortunate event you need a recompression chamber, the one you go to will be coordinated and chosen by the Diving Emergency Service (DES) ☎ 1800 088 200. Use this number for any diving accident, decompression injury/sickness, embolism, marine stings or envenomations, bites or blackouts.

If you're dealing with a situation that is immediately life-threatening (eg. where CPR or EAR is being performed on an injured diver), directly call the local emergency (ambulance) services (☎ 000) to get help as soon as possible. Listen to the operator carefully, give your exact location, phone numbers, call sign and boat or resort name and calmly explain the circumstances. Ideally, you will be able to give exact details about the patient: name, location, status, what happened, first aid given, depths, times, symptoms, times of onset, animal description, etc. Do not hang up until the operator tells you to. This is a free call, accessible 24 hours a day.

If you are at a resort, on a vessel or some other commercial facility, report the situation to the appropriate person. Do not try to take over as the staff will have locally legislated procedures to follow, which may be different from your training.

DAN

The Divers Alert Network (DAN) SE Asia-Pacific is a non-profit, membership-based diving safety association that works towards improving the safety of all divers in the Asia-Pacific Region. DAN funds hotlines, provides evacuation and insurance for divers, accident management training programs and conducts research into diving accidents and their prevention.

Go to www.diversalertnetwork.org/contact/international.asp for full details for all parts of the world. For Australia, visit www.danseap.org.

To call the US DAN ☎ 1-800-446-2671 Toll-Free, ☎ 1-919-684-2948 General Inquiries, ☎ 1-919-490-6630.

To call DAN Australia ☎ 61-3-9886-9166, Diving Emergencies DES Australia ☎ 1-800-088-200 (within Australia) or ☎ 61-8-8212-9242 (outside Australia)

They will accept collect calls in a dive emergency. DAN does not directly provide medical care; however, it does provide advice on early treatment, evacuation and hyperbaric treatment of diving-related injuries. DAN membership is reasonably priced and includes DAN TravelAssist, a membership benefit, which covers medical air evacuation from anywhere in the world for any illness or injury. For a small additional fee, divers can get secondary insurance coverage for decompression illness.

Veedub, the giant groper, hovers under the bow of the Yongala

Lady Musgrave Island and Reef is one of the many jewels in the GBR crown

Capricorn & Bunker Groups Index

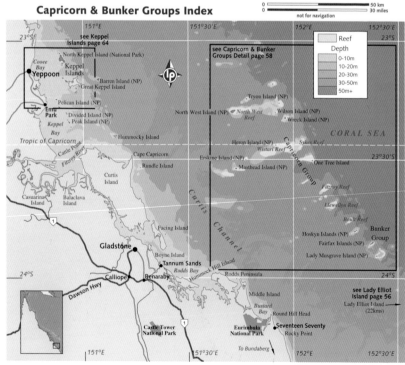

see Keppel Islands page 64

see Capricorn & Bunker Groups Detail page 58

see Lady Elliot Island page 56

0   50 km
0   30 miles
not for navigation

Reef
Depth
0-10m
10-20m
20-30m
30-50m
50m+

23°S

151°E   151°30'E   152°E   152°30'E

North Keppel Island (National Park)

Cooee Bay

Yeppoon

Keppel Islands

Barren Island (NP)

Great Keppel Island

Pelican Island (NP)

Emu Park

Divided Island (NP)

Peak Island (NP)

Keppel Bay

Tropic of Capricorn

Hummocky Island

Cattle Point

Fitzroy River

Cape Capricorn

Curtis Island

Rundle Island

Casuarina Island

Balaclava Island

Facing Island

Gladstone

Boyne Island

Tannum Sands

Rodds Bay

Calliope

Benaraby

Dawson Hwy

Castle Tower National Park

Tryon Island (NP)

North West Island (NP)

North West Reef

Wilson Island (NP)

Wreck Island (NP)

CORAL SEA

Heron Island (NP)

Sykes Reef

Wistari Reef

Erskine Island (NP)

Masthead Island (NP)

Capricorn Group

One Tree Island

Fitzroy Reef

Llewellyn Reef

Boult Reef

Hoskyn Islands (NP)

Fairfax Islands (NP)

Lady Musgrave Island (NP)

Bunker Group

Curtis Channel

Hummock Hill Island

Rodds Peninsula

Middle Island

Bustard Bay

Round Hill Head

Lady Elliot Island (22kms)

Eurimbula National Park

Seventeen Seventy

Rocky Point

To Bundaberg

23°30'S

24°S

151°E   151°30'E   152°E   152°30'E

Capricorn & Bunker Groups Dive Sites

As the southern extremity of the Great Barrier Reef (GBR), the Capricorn and Bunker reefs and islands (Lady Elliot Island, which is well south of the Bunkers, is included in them for convenience) are unusual and yet excellent representations of what the GBR and Coral Sea have to offer. There are 21 reefs – 13 with vegetated cays (Fairfax and Hoskyn have two cays each on their one reef), one with a non-vegetated cay, and five significant reefal shoals.

It is possible to camp on Lady Musgrave, Masthead and North West Islands once you've obtained permits from National Parks. Tryon Island was open to camping but has been temporarily closed to allow it to recover from a massive caterpillar invasion. Heron and Lady Elliot Islands host two of the three GBR coral cay resorts – the third is Green Island off Cairns. Heron has a research station and Marine Park Ranger base and also operates a 'wilderness' camping site for 12 guests on nearby Wilson Island.

Access to the area is limited. You fly to Lady Elliot from Bundaberg, helicopter and fast catamaran to Heron from Gladstone, and fast catamaran to Lady Musgrave from Bundaberg or Seventeen Seventy (1770). Charter and day vessels journey to the other reefs and islands, departing from Bundaberg, 1770, Gladstone and Yeppoon.

All the reefs are exposed on most low tides so there are excellent opportunities to reef walk and snorkel in addition to the varied diving around all the reefs and shoals. Humpback whales frequent the area from May through October, and manta rays and turtles are seen regularly. Thousands of birds and turtles nest on these islands, especially during the warmer months.

One Tree Island and Heron Island are home to research stations operated by Sydney and the University of Queens-

Imperial shrimps can be found on many red and white reef animal hosts

land respectively. Around all reefs, watch you don't disturb equipment set up for scientific experiments. One Tree Reef (off One Tree Island) is closed to recreational use to allow the researchers undisturbed observation.

With over 222km (120 nautical miles) of reef edges, shoal areas rich in bommies and shallow inter-reefal areas, there are plenty of diving opportunities. The resorts each have many buoyed sites and others for drift diving, while charter vessels cruise out to their favourite spots. Whatever your needs and style of diving, they will be met in this area.

Capricorn & Bunker Groups Dive Sites	GOOD SNORKELING	NOVICE	INTERMEDIATE	ADVANCED
1 LADY ELLIOT ISLAND – BLOW HOLE				•
2 LADY MUSGRAVE – ENTRANCE BOMMIE			•	
3 HERON ISLAND BOMMIE	•	•		
4 HERON ISLAND – THE GORGONIA HOLE	•	•		
5 KEPPEL ISLAND – OUTER ROCK	•	•		

Lady Elliot Island

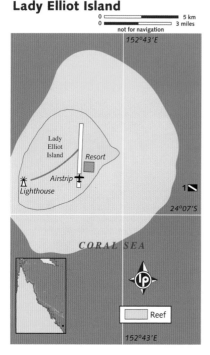

0 — 5 km
0 — 3 miles
not for navigation
152°43'E

Lady Elliot Island

Resort

Airstrip

Lighthouse

24°07'S

CORAL SEA

Reef

152°43'E

1 LADY ELLIOT ISLAND – BLOW HOLE

Location: *Outer eastern side of Lady Elliot Island*
Depth Range: *15-25m (49-82ft)*
Access: *Boat*
Expertise Rating: *Advanced*

The Lady Elliot resort provides the best resort-based diving on the GBR. The visibility is better – although access is more difficult – than many other sites. The near-circular reef has great snorkeling over the reef top and edge, and excellent dives at Lighthouse Bommies, Anchor Bommie, Coral Gardens and Encounters.

Manta rays are regulars here, along with a resident loggerhead turtle and visiting green turtles. Leopard sharks,

moray eels and schools of pelagics make this a very enjoyable area. Sea state and tide conditions often restrict boat diving, but most dives can be accessed from the beach and across the reef flat.

Lady Elliot's unusual dive site is the Blow Hole, a boat entry from the mooring buoy. You drop onto a reef terrace at 15m, where a hole suddenly appears in the reef. It is only about 6m across and drops vertically into the gloom below. Formed probably by freshwater erosion during the last ice age, or wave action as the sea level rose, this great L-shaped geological feature provides a superb dive. The hole turns at a right angle at the bottom and travels for 20m before opening out into another hole about 6m wide and 3m high. This opening in the wall is an exciting dive in itself, as it rises from 25m to 15m, running off both directions away from the blow hole.

After exiting the hole at 25m, the bottom of the wall to the right offers great caves, nooks and crannies occupied by anemones, hard and soft corals, magnificent gorgonians and many fish. Keep a regular look out into the blue as passing manta, eagle and bull rays sometimes accompany the reef sharks and turtles that are regulars here. Silver tip sharks also sometimes appear. Other regular sightings include lionfish, wobbegong sharks and schooling blubberlips, while wrasse and banded coral shrimp provide cleaner services to the fish here.

During summer the hole can completely fill with bait fish, attracting predators that come crashing through the masses. Once you're in the hole, look up for superb silhouette shots and more photo opportunities as you hit the bottom of the turn. Feather stars, black, turret and soft corals all add colour to frame your shots in the tunnels. This is definitely a wide-angle lens dive that requires a computer and multi-level tables. Bring a light to enhance your discoveries.

To gaze up into the Lady Elliot blowhole is a true buzz for divers

The Lady Musgrave Reef entrance provides excellent dive opportunities

Capricorn & Bunker Groups Detail

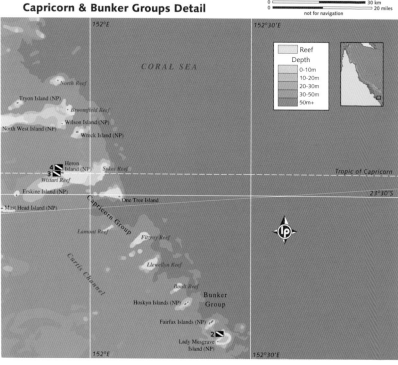

2 LADY MUSGRAVE – ENTRANCE BOMMIE

Location: *5km (3 miles) from island, outside entrance to lagoon, north-west side of reef*
Depth Range: *5-22m (16-72ft)*
Access: *Boat*
Expertise Rating: *Intermediate*

Lady Musgrave, one of the 13 vegetated coral cay reefs in the Capricorn and Bunker groups, is a good example of them all. It has some excellent diving along its back edge, near the island (where you can camp), in the Coral Gardens, on the Battery Bommies and Manta Ray Bommie, and at the front at The Drop-Offs. The pontoon anchored in the lagoon is an excellent base for great snorkeling to be done at this reef.

When the tide is rising or slack, the Entrance Bommie is the standout in this group of dive sites. Tides cause strong currents running in or out. A roll entry from the boat drops you onto the top of this large rich coral head. Dive to a maximum depth of 22m, then make your way up and around the bommie. Numerous small nooks and crannies and overhangs provide lots of places for small marine life to hang out.

Porites, or boulder coral, is the primary constructor of this head, with large colonies of plate and staghorn now covering much of its surface. Mushroom and brain corals are also common among the soft corals, which are well interspersed throughout the site.

The constant passing parade of fish include surgeons, painted flutemouths, clown triggerfish, batfish, sergeant majors, butterflyfish and coral trout. Clouds of blue damsels and passing schools of trevally add to the movement. If you are lucky, a lionfish, potato cod or giant moray eels may show up.

Barramundi cod, big eyes and cardinalfish can be seen hiding in and beneath the overhangs.

Less common are manta rays and sea snakes, with turtles being more regular visitors, sometimes resting under an overhang. Please don't disturb them, they can slam into you or your buddy, causing you to lose your mouthpiece or mask.

The sea snakes, if seen, are best observed from a distance – they are highly venomous and inquisitive, but harmless if you don't annoy them. Look for cuttlefish too – their constantly changing colours add to the kaleidoscope effect of the site. Parrotfish crunch at the coral and algae and at night can be found resting in their mucous cocoons. Whitetip and blacktip reef sharks can appear as well.

Yellow flute-mouths are rarely seen, voracious predators on small fish

The Turtle's Precarious Birth

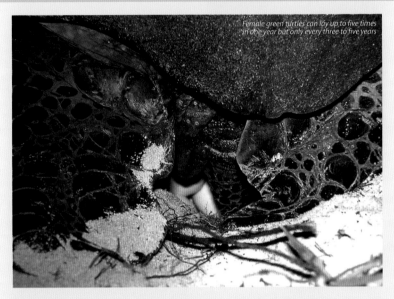

Female green turtles can lay up to five times in one year but only every three to five years

Six species of marine turtle are found in the GBR and Coral Sea waters; most common are green, hawksbill and loggerheads. These species feed and mate in the waters around the islands, and the nesting females can be seen ashore at night. You can also see them from the air, from boats or when diving throughout the GBR.

A nesting female lumbering out of the water is a wonderful sight. Once on land, she first digs a body pit and then an egg chamber. If the sand temperature and moisture content is right, she will lay between 50 and 150 eggs. She then buries the whole pit area, including the egg chamber, and leaves. She will lay up to five times in one year, but only every three to five years.

Incubation takes about six or seven weeks, after which the hatchlings dig up the surface and wait until it is dark and cool (either at night or after a rain shower) before emerging. Sand temperature affects the outcomes of each nesting – hotter sand (above 30°C/86°F) results in more females, 30°C produces both males and females, and below 30°C, more males.

The dash across the beach to the sea is dangerous. Gulls and other predatory birds will swoop in for a meal. Once the turtle escapes and reaches the relative safety of the reef edge and deeper water, it becomes prey to sharks and larger fish that will happily feast on it. If it survives this start of its journey, the turtle cruises the open ocean until it is about dinner-plate size, when it returns to start living in reef waters. Adult turtles regularly travel thousands of kilometres, so turtles that are protected in Australia may be hunted and eaten in Indonesia.

If you see a turtle, consider yourself lucky and be respectful of this rare experience. Don't shine flashlights on, walk in front of, or go closer than 15m (50ft) to nesting turtles. Always be slow and careful. Never touch or hang on to turtles underwater, as this stresses them greatly especially if they are on their way to the surface to breathe.

3 HERON ISLAND BOMMIE

Location: *Between harbour mouth and western end of reef – buoyed.*
Depth Range: *3-25m (10-82ft)*
Access: *Boat*
Expertise Rating: *Novice*

Heron Island is a richly vegetated coral cay and important nesting site for green turtles, black noddy terns and wedge-tailed shearwaters with a resort, research station and Marine Parks ranger base. It is serviced by helicopters (30 minutes) and high speed catamaran (2½ hours), from Gladstone.

There are more than 10 regularly dived sites with canyons, gullies, bommies, walls, drifts and sandy floors. The Bommie is one of the most famous dive sites in the world, as this area has been seen in almost every film, documentary or story ever made on the GBR, and was one of the first commercially dived sites.

It is a very reliable site with good access. Schools of hussars and sweetlip, whitetip reef sharks, moray eels and parrotfish swim against a superb backdrop of staghorn coral banks and four large (and many smaller) boulder coral heads. This is also the local cleaning station and is a great place to photograph a cleaner wrasse inside a trout's mouth.

Overhangs and several tunnels provide ideal sites for turret coral, with their brilliant yellow polyps, especially at night. Some fish can be seen at night, sleeping in the small caves and overhangs. Be careful not to disturb them.

Manta and eagle rays are occasional visitors but are hesitant to come close. You need to keep a good eye out into the blue to see them or turtles. Often the first divers to the site will see resting turtles at the base of the coral heads, along with wobbegong sharks.

Heron Island's Bommie is one of the best fish dives ever

An anchoring boat broke the top off the main head in the '70s and the constant diving pressure has removed most of the fragile corals from the site, although more diver sensitivity seems to be allowing it to slowly return.

After a giant stride entry from the boat, follow the mooring line down to an old admiralty anchor and then to the largest head at 6m. You can easily spend your whole dive here or go exploring down the sand slope and around the smaller heads. The current can be uncomfortable on big tide runs. It is a great snorkel site, but can get a bit crowded if the semi-sub shows up at the same time.

4 HERON ISLAND – THE GORGONIA HOLE

Location: *Due north of resort, on reef slope*
Depth Range: *3-25m (10-82ft)*
Access: *Boat*
Expertise Rating: *Novice*

The Gorgonian Hole is a reef-edge boat dive with an excellent variety of small soft corals and, like all the sites at Heron, the fish are very familiar with divers.

You dive down the reef slope through several boulder corals and gully structures rich with plate staghorns, into a hole-like amphitheatre and then into a broken reef edge, which has numerous small caves, gullies and great coral cover. The base of the slope (at 20m), breaks into a sand rubble floor with isolated coral patches. It's best to stay above this, where the life and scenery is much better.

It is a popular dive site, with a range of soft corals. Further east along the wall, you'll see some larger fan corals and plate staghorn coral colonies in the shallows. Fern-like stinging hydroids are quite common and if you are lucky, you'll see an octopus, shark, manta or eagle ray.

Turtles are regulars, especially in summer during mating and nesting periods. Feather stars and their small commensal gobies, shrimp and crabs provide more splashes of colour as the basslets and damsels swarm in and out of the corals. Sea fans reach out into the current, while smaller nudibranchs, worms and crabs are seen in close. Trevally, hussars and sweetlip are common. The site suits all types of divers and photographers and is generally safe. If there is a strong current run you may get to see several other nearby sites during a drift dive.

Commensal gobies take the same colour as their hosts – here a crinoid or feather star

Red gorgonian fan soft corals with polyps out, filter the currents for food
Photo: Neville Zell

5 KEPPEL ISLANDS – OUTER ROCK

Location: *Due east of North Keppel Island*
Depth Range: *4-22m (13-72ft)*
Access: *Boat*
Expertise Rating: *Novice*

Featuring two large islands, several smaller islands and rocks, the Keppels area has some great dives on fringing and 'veneer' reef communities, whereby the reef life grows a veneer over island rock, inviting fish life in to occupy the site. The best dives are at Outer Rock, Barren Island, Man & Wife Rocks and Egg Rock.

The entry at Outer Rock drops to 8m, next to some superb ridges that are rich in hard and soft coral. You can dive down and over the ridges to the northeast, turn west over to the point and then back up into the shallows for your safety stop.

The ridge is known as Snake Paradise due to the resident population of olive sea snakes, which generally appear less inquisitive than fellow snakes because they are so busy searching for food. They may check you out when they start for the surface to breathe. Let them do their thing and don't annoy them.

There are many gutters to explore, some with sea cucumbers on the bottom and side ledges. A careful look under the ledges may yield a painted crayfish, sea star or nudibranch sighting. Damsels, butterflyfish, sergeant majors, fusiliers, anemones, wrasse and

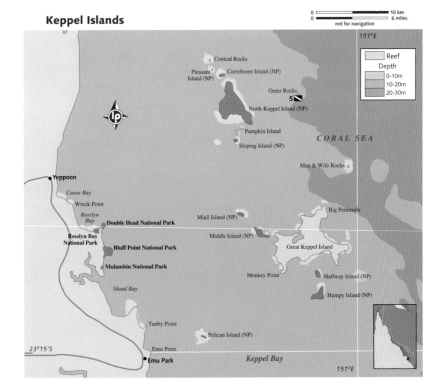

Keppel Islands

0 — 10 km
0 — 6 miles
not for navigation

151°E

Reef
Depth
0-10m
10-20m
20-30m

Conical Rocks
Pleasant Island (NP)   Corroboree Island (NP)
Outer Rocks
5
North Keppel Island (NP)
Pumpkin Island
Sloping Island (NP)   *CORAL SEA*
Man & Wife Rocks
Yeppoon
Cooee Bay
Wreck Point
Rosslyn Bay   Double Head National Park   Miall Island (NP)   Big Peninsula
Rosslyn Bay National Park
Bluff Point National Park   Middle Island (NP)   Great Keppel Island
Mulambin National Park
Monkey Point   Halfway Island (NP)
Shoal Bay   Humpy Island (NP)
Tanby Point
23°15'S   Pelican Island (NP)
Emu Point
Emu Park   *Keppel Bay*
151°E

parrotfish are always present here. You'll also see coral trout, wobbegong sharks, stingrays and the occasional Maori wrasse. Green and loggerhead turtles are also regular visitors, along with long toms, Spanish mackerel, and greasy and honeycomb cod.

The snorkeling and safety stop area is closer to the island, over the staghorn coral patches and up to the rocks, where a moray eel hangs out. Be careful not to rub the oyster-encrusted rocks that are covered with water at high tides – they can cut you badly.

Stinging hydroids, stonefish and lionfish are dangers to be aware of, but aren't usually a problem. Best times of year tend to be late winter to early summer when visibility is better, and winds and waves are milder.

Coral Bleaching

Bleached coral goes white as the zooxanthellae are expelled

Coral bleaching occurs when corals are under severe stress, which can be induced by many factors. Extreme temperatures and increased UV rays are the two most important, but disease, chemicals, salinity and exposure to air and rain at extreme low tides can also be significant. Human influences on coastal run-off, water quality and low salinity effects can also contribute to coral bleaching.

Bleaching occurs when corals shed some or all of their zooxanthellae, the single-celled plant that lives in the coral animal tissue. These plants produce too much oxygen, which becomes toxic to the animal that then expels them. The colony appears to go white, but if you examine it closely, you'll see a thin layer of animal tissue, like a sheath, over the white calcium carbonate skeleton. Corals can recover if the stress was not extreme and if the few remaining zooxanthellae reproduce and re-establish the symbiotic relationship.

Research shows bleaching to be a regular natural phenomenon that can worsen in El Nino years, with fluctuating water temperatures and tides. Recently, on the GBR's inshore fringing reef systems, a major bleaching event was linked to high temperatures, low tides, rainfall, coastal run-off and very calm conditions. Almost 90% of inshore reefs had significant bleaching in 1998, and 25% had more than half their corals affected. The offshore reef systems of the GBR and Coral Sea had minimal or no bleaching recorded, probably due to less water from the mainland and more water movement, lessening the hot water accumulation seen in shallower coastal waters. Six bleaching events have been documented on the GBR in the last 20 years, with anecdotal evidence indicating that more have occurred in the past. There is now major evidence that coral bleaching is becoming more regular due to global warming.

Swain Reefs

0 ————————— 20 km
0 ————————— 10 miles
not for navigation

152°30'E

Reef

21-274

Distant Cay

Elusive Reef

21-281

21-289

21-295

21-296

■6
East Cay   21°30'S

21-468
21-477   21-558

Bacchi Cay
Twin Cay   21-560

Frigate Cay
Detour Reef   Half-Tide
                Reef

                    Blu Lion Reef

Emperor
Reef
                         Beacon Reef
Pike Reef
Gannet Cay   *Caradus Passage*   22°S
                            Wade Reef

Chesterman   *Horseshoe Reef*
Reef
                    Sanctuary
                     Reef
Abrahams   *Hook Reef*
Reef

                Sandshoe Reef

                    Sweetlip Reef

                Hixson Cay
            South Hixson Cay
152°30'E

From staghorns to waves – the diversity
of life challenges all divers on the GBR

Swain Reefs Dive Sites

Olive sea snakes are common in some Swain Reef areas

The southern extension of the wilderness and adventure diving areas of the Great Barrier Reef (GBR) are called the Swain Reefs, or Swains to the locals. They are only serviced by charter boats with roving permits. The complex is 100km to 250km (62 miles to 155 miles) from the coast and has over 270 reefs, more than 25 with cays. The reefs range in size from a few hundred metres across to over 20km (12 miles) in length. Most average around 4km (2.5 miles), providing thousands of exciting, exploratory and adventure dive sites. The reefs are rich with life and the cays are important as protected sea bird rookeries and resting areas. There's an automatic weather station on one of the cays.

Today, parts of the Swain Reefs are used for preservation areas, national park, commercial trawling (some western areas only), fishing, recreational use and research. In many areas fishing has depleted numerous fish species such as trout, cod and sweetlip. The most recent marine park zoning will go a small way towards allowing regeneration of fish stocks.

As much of the area is unexplored, each dive boat takes divers to their favoured spots, usually associated with a good anchorage in the prevailing weather. There are many anchorage sites so even if there are a few boats out, it is unlikely you will see them, as the area is so large. Depending on which harbour you started from and how long you have, you will probably cover either the northern or southern section. Either way, you will get excellent uncrowded diving and snorkeling. Usually there is no set itinerary – your trip will be determined by weather and the whim of the group.

Swain Reefs Dive Sites	GOOD SNORKELING	NOVICE	INTERMEDIATE	ADVANCED
6 EAST CAY	•	•		

Good walls, excellent reef edges, gutters, drop-offs, tunnels, swim-throughs, ledges, terraces, caves, overhangs and large coral heads occur throughout the area. In short, virtually any coral reef feature imaginable can be found. Shallow lagoonal reeftops and sandy floors host large staghorn thickets and many species of shells can be seen, especially at night. Most of the area is less than 30m (98ft) deep between the reefs, so there is not much opportunity for deep diving and visibility can be reduced during rough weather and big tides.

Sea snakes are common at some reefs and sharks, turtles and rays can be seen throughout. Fish diversity is high. The usual suites of inshore species abound, with outer-edge species becoming more common as you go east. Whales, whale sharks, dolphins and leatherback turtles have all been reported, so keep your eyes peeled.

Shipwreck remains can be seen on some reeftops but many other wrecks are yet to be found. Tales of bravery and sadness abound from ships that sailed, dived and fished this complex including many of the early divers who explored these areas in the '60s.

sandy floored areas in between. Back in the more sheltered areas you'll find rich staghorn thickets and small coral patches. The bommies reach from sand at 20-25m to the surface.

By diving from a dinghy you can enter the water on either the outside for a drift dive, or in amongst the gutters if the weather or current is not suitable to drift. Go to your planned depth and work your way up and around the complex of structures. It is usual to see larger fish like trout, cod and whitetip reef sharks in the gutters. Small angelfish, butterflyfish, damsels and surgeonfish are common, with wrasse and parrotfish zipping around as well. Sea snakes are common – they should be treated with respect and left alone.

Feather stars sit up on the fan corals catching passing food. At night it is easier to photograph molluscs on the sand as they are seldom seen any other time. This site is good for wide-angle photography on most days but is always a great macro area as well. Numerous varied sites provide for a great snorkel or dive on this reef.

Silvertip sharks are inquisitive for short times only

6 | EAST CAY

Location: *Northeast of back reef slope and bommie fields*
Depth Range: *1-25m (3-82ft)*
Access: *Boat*
Expertise Rating: *Novice*

Boat operators like this reef due to the easy-access anchorage and small sand cay, demonstrating much of what the Swains offer. It's an attractive diving reef thanks to the variety of coral structures, especially on the north and eastern ends of the reef. Complex bommies and gutters provide great swim-throughs with

What is a coral?

Look carefully at coral communities to see how diverse they are

Coral is a popular term used for many bottom-dwelling animals. The four main ones are, in evolutionary sequence: hydroids (or stinging corals), anthozoans (hard or stony corals), black corals, and gorgonians (including soft corals).

Hard corals are the primary reef-builders and these animals have a major waste problem. As hard corals grow, they dump their waste calcium carbonate outside their tissues. The pattern in which these crystals are laid down leads to the different shapes of hard coral skeletons seen when the coral dies and rots, or is eaten. Enormous numbers of single-celled plants, called zooxanthellae, live inside the coral tissue and absorb carbon dioxide, waste phosphates and nitrates from the coral (other animals discard the waste through their urine and faeces). They also collect sunlight and produce sugars and oxygen that the coral, uses. During this symbiotic process, calcium carbonate becomes a waste product and has to be dumped. Voila! A coral skeleton.

Each coral animal is known as a polyp, with a sac-like stomach, a ring of tentacles around the top and a mouth in the centre. They may be a single solitary coral, or a colony formed by thousands of polyps. Internal vertical ridges in the stomach determine the shape of holes in the coral skeleton, increase the surface area to help digest food and also carry the gonads.

Coral tentacles are packed with stinging cells called nematocysts. These act like mini-darts, injecting toxin into prey. Corals are farmers by day, when their tentacles are retracted, allowing the zooxanthellae to absorb sunlight. They become active carnivores at night when the tentacles expand and wave around to capture any blundering creature. Prey is taken into the sac-like gut and digested. Hard waste is ejected out the central mouth, while digested food is shared amongst polyps in the colony and other waste is used by the zooxanthellae. Corals are vicious killers and will engulf one another through slow overgrowing, or by sending out sweeper tentacles, which kill or digest neighbouring corals. This is a slow process (taking months or even years) but is very effective in the measured and purposeful life of a coral.

Soft corals have multiples of eight tentacles (hard corals are multiples of six) and usually a fleshy (filled with spicules or little spines in the tissues), horny or semi-rigid skeleton, such as in sea fans and whips. There are many other corals such as the rare black, red and even 'freshwater corals', belonging to quite different groups of animals than those well known from the Indo-Pacific reefs.

Satellites allow imagery showing the size and extent of parts of the GBR – here the Whitsundays and Tee, Hardline and Pompey Reefs
Photo: NASA

Blue pullers are great to watch as they dash out to pluck plankton from the waters nearby

Pompey Complex

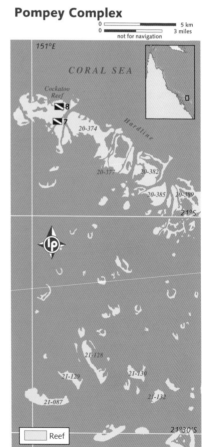

0 — 5 km
0 — 3 miles
not for navigation

151°E

CORAL SEA

Cockatoo Reef

8
7

Hardline

20-374

20-377   20-382

20-385   20-389

21°S

21-128

21-129   21-130

21-087   21-132

Reef

21°30'S

Pompey Complex Dive Sites

Nudibranchs always challenge the macro-photographer

long, others are square-shaped, up to 100 sq km (40 sq miles). The reeftops have many intricately shaped, closed and shallow lagoons and some are almost flat, abraded coral/algal surfaces. Between the reefs are channels up to 90m (295ft) deep and 200m (656ft) across. They are u-shaped and were probably formed during the last ice age. Some of the outflows and many reefs appear as deltas from the air. Their sides are vertical walls that fall to a smooth limestone floor.

The tide change inshore of the Pompeys is the largest on the east coast of Australia – almost 7m (22ft) – which means an enormous amount of water passes through four times each day (on the two rising and two falling tides). It is usual to see tide runs in excess of 15km/h (9mph), which causes whirlpools and rising water that is 10cm to 20cm (4in to 8in) higher than the adjacent reef. Tide heights range from 7m (22ft) inside and 4m (13ft) outside of the Pompeys – some of the highest tide ranges on coral reefs in the world.

As you might expect, the marine life here is rich and hardy, able to withstand intense water speeds. This is the most southern point to find the giant clam (Tridacna gigas). Sea snakes are common throughout much of the area, but where and when they appear is unpredictable. The currents ensure great populations of pelagic fish in the gyre and current lee eddy areas.

Between the Swain Reefs and Whitsundays is a continuation of the southern wilderness adventure diving area. The Pompey Complex (which includes the Tee Line and Hardline) has blue holes, u-shaped channels with strong currents, sheer walls, water 'falls,' whirlpools, and an unbelievable diversity of reefs. Navigation is dangerous for many vessels, so the area remains under-explored. If you get the chance to get here – take it!

About 150 reefs make up this complex, which is about 200km (124 miles) north-to-south, 90km (56 miles) west-to-east and up to 185km (115 miles) from the mainland coast. Most have no names and are recognised only by their numbers on the Marine Park Zoning Plan maps. Some are 20km (12 miles)

Pompey Complex Dive Sites	GOOD SNORKELING	NOVICE	INTERMEDIATE	ADVANCED
7 COCKATOO REEF – THE SOUTHERN WALL		•		•
8 COCKATOO REEF – BLUE HOLE		•	•	

At least three blue holes occur in the complex. These are usually old caves that formed during the last ice age and collapsed as the waters rose. Just off the outer edge of these reefs is an old submerged reef front, which remains to be explored.

7 COCKATOO REEF – THE SOUTHERN WALL

Location: *Channel edge of reef on southern side*
Depth Range: *1-27m+ (3-90ft+)*
Access: *Boat*
Expertise Rating: *Advanced*

An adrenaline rush. You need to know exactly when the tide stops running to get into the water here. Enjoy your dive and as soon as you see all the fish turn to face the changed current direction, end your dive! Know your plan and buddy well, and carry your safety sausage.

Vertical channel walls plummet from the reeftop to the scoured limestone-rock channel floor at 40m to 80m. The mid-reef wall has smaller life adapted to intense water flows. Hard corals, soft corals, sponges, coralline algae and many small fish abound. Life inside the caves and overhangs tend to be larger. Schools of pelagics also flash through.

Once you reach either a channel into the lagoon, or the end of the reef channel, drift and pop around into the lagoon or back reef area, before a rising tide, where another world awaits. Rich staghorn beds and coral gardens, abraded coralline algal surfaces and many grazing fish are the norm.

Sharks, barracuda, rays and mackerel circle in the eddies, waiting for unsuspecting fish. On the lagoon floor, many shells come out, especially at night, and feeding sea cucumbers and goatfish are common.

8 COCKATOO REEF – BLUE HOLE

Location: *Inside lagoon*
Depth Range: *1-30m (3-98ft)*
Access: *Boat*
Expertise Rating: *Novice*

This blue hole in the reef top has the classic shape of a perfectly round coral rim that exposes at low tide and has a blue interior. It sits in a shallow 10m lagoon, with a vertical wall to 10m outside and 7m inside, that slopes inward forming a conical pool with smooth sand/sediment sides to 30m.

Snorkeling around the 200m diameter rim is fun, with rich staghorn corals of the wall. Once inside the rim, you'll find a mix of coral species with staghorns becoming more dominant. All coral stops at about 15m as it becomes buried in sediment. It is a fascinating experience to dive in what was an old cave thousands of years ago that has since collapsed, forming this pool.

Fish life is limited inside, presumably due to lower water exchange, but you'll still see stripeys, sweetlip, trout, damsels, butterflyfish, wrasse, parrotfish and angels. Outside is a 'normal' lagoonal reef edge supporting rich life, especially in the small overhangs and caves. There you'll see worms, crabs, crayfish, shells, soft and hard corals and sea cucumbers.

Isolated coral heads offer enormous diversity of life for the observant diver.

Wall dives allow divers to see more without risking reef damage

Whitsunday Islands & Nearby Reefs

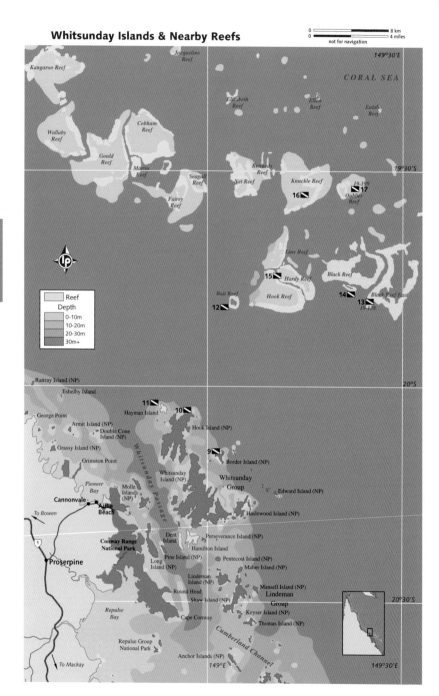

Whitsunday Islands & Nearby Reefs Dive Sites

Aerial view of the magnificent Whitehaven Beach in the Whitsunday Islands
Photo: Manfred Gottschalk

the principle departure point for dive cruises to the Whitsunday Islands and nearby mid-shelf to outer Great Barrier Reef. On the resort islands, which range from backpacker-style hostels to five-star hotels, there are ample resort-style activities including golf, hiking, tennis, windsurfing and dining.

Resort and mainland dive centres provide diver training facilities and trips. Specialised dive boats offer live-aboard dive cruises to many of the mid-shelf and some outer-reef dive sites, while day dives to the islands and reef are also available. You may wish to charter an aircraft and fly between sites!

You can dive the local island fringing reefs or the GBR proper – between 65km (40 miles) and 140km (85 miles) east of Airlie Beach – which has a superb range of dive sites. Humpback whales pass through in winter and other reef life is rich and diverse. Reef structures are excellent with great walls, caverns, overhangs, coral gardens and lagoons. Strong currents from the big tides are not a problem, as dive operators know where to go, regardless of the conditions.

More than 100 continental islands make up the Whitsundays, including the Cumberland Group and the coast from Mackay to Bowen. The Whitsundays appeared as islands when the seas rose after the last ice age, drowning the valleys between the islands. This area is now a tourism hot spot for sailing, island hopping, holidaying and scuba diving.

Island dive sites are generally at the northern end of the Whitsunday Group and can be quite spectacular when the tides and weather are favourable; however, it is the nearby areas of the mid-shelf and outer Great Barrier Reef (GBR) that offer the best local sites.

Accommodations and primary exit points to the Coral Sea and Whitsunday Islands are at Airlie Beach and Shute Harbour. Abel Point Marina at Airlie Beach is

Whitsunday Islands & Nearby Reefs Dive Sites	GOOD SNORKELING	NOVICE	INTERMEDIATE	ADVANCED
9 BORDER ISLAND – CATARAN BAY	•	•		
10 HOOK ISLAND MANTA RAY BAY	•	•		
11 HAYMAN ISLAND – BLUE PEARL BAY	•	•		
12 BAIT REEF – STEPPING STONES			•	
13 SVANE'S REEF – HELL DRIFT		•		•
14 LITTLE BLACK REEF – LAGOON		•	•	
15 HARDY REEF – FANTASEA DRIFT		•	•	
16 KNUCKLE REEF – WALKING STICK		•		•
17 JUST MAGIC ON REEF 19-119				•

Clams offer great close-up experiences for divers and photographers

9 BORDER ISLAND – CATARAN BAY

Location: *North side Border Island*
Access: *Boat*
Depth Range: *0-15m (0-49ft)*
Expertise Rating: *Novice*

Border Island is the furthest Whitsunday island from the coast, giving it generally better visibility than the inshore islands. The winds can be strong, but the water stays calm and enjoyable for snorkeling or diving.

Turtles are regulars and during whale season you may hear the 'squeaky door' songs of passing humpbacks, but you need to listen carefully. Reef sharks are common but are easily spooked and will quickly disappear.

Large schools of baitfish sometimes appear and attract predatory trevally, queenfish and mackerel swooping in for a meal. Fusiliers are common, as are the many smaller reef fish that abound near the coral.

You can find excellent walls and overhangs and the areas around and under large bommies provide great hiding spots for coral trout and sweetlip. The shallow areas are dotted with numerous clams in various shades of blue, brown, aqua and purple. Christmas tree worms are also common, as are many other small organisms if you take the time to see them. This is an ideal site for macrophotography.

On the shallow areas of the bommie tops there is more soft and hard coral, along with large colonies of stinging coral, so beware of their fiery sting. Parrotfish graze on the exposed reef surface and pairs of butterflyfish dart around between the staghorn coral colonies. As you finish your dive, take a drift snorkel or swim over the shallows to see how different these sites are to other reef types. Snorkeling is best in this area at mid-to-low tide.

10 HOOK ISLAND – MANTA RAY BAY

Location: *Northeast end of Hook Island*
Depth Range: *0-15m (0-49ft)*
Access: *Boat*
Expertise Rating: *Novice*

As one of the more popular bays for snorkeling and diving in the Whitsundays, Manta Ray Bay has mooring limitations. The fish are numerous and familiar with humans – look for Fat Albert, the resident Maori wrasse, for proof. He weighs about 100kg and has bright aqua markings around his face. Smaller females accompany him wherever he goes. Interestingly, when Fat Albert dies, the largest female will frantically change sex and take his place as the dominant male.

Underwater terrain consists of large bommies extending from 15m to the surface with overhangs, small caves and clumps of corals on a muddy sandy floor. Stinging coral and staghorns give primary cover. Friendly batfish abound with fusiliers, sergeant majors and masses of planktiverous (plankton-eating) fish more common near shore.

The blue staghorn thickets here are probably the best to be seen in the Whitsunday Islands area. Soft corals, occasional black coral trees and gorgonians can also be seen. If you venture to the rocky end of the bay, look for some of the big splits occuring in the rocks.

Cleaner stations are common and if you are lucky you may see a cleaner swim into Fat Albert's mouth to clean his teeth and gills. On good days this is a great area for macro or super wide-angle, close-up photography. Upon finishing the dive, beware of the boat traffic on the surface.

Lower visibility sites still offer great reef life for the observant diver.

Sex lives of fish

If you ever asked a fish what sex it was, it would be important to add, 'I mean, right now.' Many fish start life as one sex then change irreversibly during their growth – some from male to female and others female to male. The cleaner wrasse is a good example. A male has a harem of females; once you remove the male, the largest female (which the male dominated until now) turns into a male. She/he now dominates all the females and if 'he' is removed, the next largest female changes to male, and on it goes.

The anemonefish has a different system: one large female lives in a 'family' made up of a male and several juveniles. If she is removed, the male becomes female and the juveniles step up the sex ladder as well.

Obviously, fishing can negatively affect breeding populations. If, for example, a large male coral trout is removed, following the rules of nature, a female then must change sex younger and smaller than it normally would, making reproduction less effective.

When it comes to parenting: fish employ every conceivable method. Some spawn in the surface waters (pelagic spawning), while others spawn on the bottom by attaching their eggs to the substrate and caring for them until they hatch (demersal spawning). Seahorse females lay their eggs in the male's front pouch, where they stay until they hatch. Some sharks give birth to live young, others lay eggs. If you are a tiger shark, your siblings may even eat you before you are born!

11 HAYMAN ISLAND – BLUE PEARL BAY

Location: *West side of Hayman Island*
Depth Range: *1-15m (3-49ft)*
Access: *By boat or from beach after boat delivery*
Expertise Rating: *Novice*

The Whitsunday Islands are surrounded by an abundance of rich fringing reefs, sandy and rocky shores and mangroves. The northern islands tend to have clearer waters, except for those outside to the east, although the reefs are generally the same species composition. Other popular nearby sites include **Maureen's Cove, Manta Ray Bay** and **Butterfly Bay**. Snorkeling at any of these island beaches, coves and reefs is a delight.

Blue Pearl Bay offers fringing reef diving at its best. At low tide, visibility is often reduced but the diversity of sea life remains outstanding. Large coral heads rise from the muddy sand floor from 7m to 15m and are topped with delightful aggregations of sergeant majors, blue pullers and other damselfish which dash about the stinging and plate coral colonies.

A resident tasselated wobbegong shark is hard to find because of its camouflaged skin and habit of lying under small overhangs. Batfish, harlequin tuskfish and parrotfish are abundant

The Bait Reef Stepping Stones are a stunning array of coral heads
Photo: Craig Lamotte

with the territorial damsel likely to rush out and peck your hair as you approach its territory.

Small caves, overhangs and crevices through the bommies occur but few are safe to swim through. The sizes are restrictive and the silt stirs up easily. Keep your buoyancy right and off the bottom.

During the day, some of the coral here have incredibly long polyps, especially the long-tentacled mushroom corals – look for commensal shrimp among their tentacles. Anemones are common, hosting several species of clownfish. Observant divers will be rewarded with nudibranchs, carnation corals and other unusual sightings.

As you finish your dive in the shallows watch out for the many stinging coral colonies. Boat traffic can be a worry so always be aware of where and how you ascend.

12 BAIT REEF – STEPPING STONES

Location: *Southwest back of Bait Reef*
Depth Range: *2-30m+ (7-100ft+)*
Access: *Boat*
Expertise Rating: *Novice to advanced*

Bait Reef is the first reef you'll encounter as you head out from the Whitsunday Islands and has several diving areas including The Maze, Cluster of Four, Coral Gardens, Hawaii and The Looking Glass. All are within the Stepping Stones, a series of 17 flat-topped bommies rising from 50m to sometimes be exposed at low tide. There are seven more round-topped bommies submerged. There are canyons, caves, swim-throughs, walls and a vast array of corals and sea life and it is a favourite of underwater photographers. It's so large, you could dive here for a week and still not see it all.

Whitsunday Islands offer great beaches and fringing reefs with sheltered anchorages

Drift diving at dusk is a buzz that's hard to beat – and sometimes scary!

Drop in near one of the bommies to 20m, only a few metres up-current from the shallow coral edge. Great swim-throughs, splits, gullies, overhangs and crevices are all around. Below them a sand slope starts at 15m to 23m and slopes away past 30m. Lower down, the rubble slope has less hard coral cover, rather you'll find colonies of spiky soft coral and sea fans.

As you are almost always surrounded by bommies, you can get caught in lots of amazing eddy effects. It is great fun to use the eddies to swoosh around to the other side of a bommie, then wait for them to change direction and take you back, or just hover in the lee.

A great scattering of staghorn clumps leads to thickets on the shallower la-goon side, and soft corals decorate the ridges below the bommies. Look in the thickets for foxface, anemones, butter-flyfish and angelfish. Mushroom corals lie under the coral trout, sweetlip and whip corals. Occasionally you will see a turtle asleep under an overhang or perhaps feeding on the edges of the bommies.

Swim-throughs, gullies, overhangs and a rich set of reeftops provide good diving and ideal fish habitats. Feather stars give a splash of colour and schools of fusiliers hover in the current, feed-ing and waiting for night when they become more active.

This is a great macro site and, on clear days, wide-angle opportunities are fantastic.

13 SVANE'S REEF (REEF 19-138) – HELL DRIFT

Location: *Entire northeast side of Reef 19-138*
Depth Range: *0-20m+ (0-66ft+)*
Access: *Boat*
Expertise Rating: *Advanced*

This site has an exciting parachute entry to test your buoyancy and general diving skills. Get yourself organised, collect your buddy and swim over to the vertical reef edge before you begin the drift along it.

In parts of the reef this top is heavily reticulated with gullies and grooves, giving superb coral coverage for hovering fish taking refuge from predators and the current.

At the reef edge drop down the wall to your planned depth and be very careful you don't go past it – it is very easy to do so. The life drops off quickly after 20m. Gorgonian fans, whips and sponges with clinging feather stars are colourful features.

Large fish species like trout, sweetlip and cod are common, and keep an eye out for pelagic mackerel and trevally zooming past as well.

Up the wall and in the shallows, masses of smaller planktivores flit about and, if you're lucky, you'll spot turtles cruising by.

A great way to dive this site is to get to a comfortable depth, stay close to the wall, relax and let it all go by while keeping your buddy in view. There is ample life of all kinds and interesting structural features to give you a great dive for minimal effort.

As you finish your dive in the shallows at Turtle Point, watch the fish behaviour during your safety stop, then surface and swim out to the boat.

Overhangs and crevices allow creatures and divers to escape the currents

Feeding damsels create a cloud above a staghorn clump

14 LITTLE BLACK REEF – LAGOON

Location: *West side of reef*
Lagoon Depth: *20m (66ft); Outside: 40m+ (130ft+)*
Access: *Boat*
Lagoon Expertise Rating: *Novice; advanced outside*

Little Black Reef's sandy lagoon floor – at 10m to 20m – has patches of staghorn coral and sea cucumbers, and is a great easy dive or training area. The Elephant Rock wall dive, on the outside of the lagoon, is definitely for advanced divers, much like **Svane's Hell Drift** dive.

Parrotfish abound and the reeftops offer great snorkeling. Inside the lagoon, stingrays are often seen in the sand, and a large bommie provides some good all-round diving.

The lagoon walls are mainly vertical with interesting life and some under-cuts and overhangs. Advanced divers can drift the walls and slopes outside the entrance as part of their lagoon dive. To the south of the mooring is a great night dive along the wall, into the notch and swim-through.

Watch for the solitary daytime mushroom coral that looks like an anemone sitting on the bottom. They often have transparent shrimps living among the tentacles.

Outside the lagoon, diving is current driven and tidally dependent. There is the potential to go deep quickly if you don't watch your depth – keep your eye on the wall and reef edge. Good corals and fish, overhangs, walls and sand flowing down the rubble slope make this a great dive.

Visibility varies from 10m to 25m; currents can be quick so trust your dive operator to pick the safest and best times.

drops you up-current to the north or south, depending on the tide, at a buoy with a descent line. You drift with the tide back to the pontoon until you hit the mooring and diver ascent line. All dives are escorted and a lifeguard sits high on the end of the pontoon keeping a lookout for snorkelers and divers.

Small bommies provide great surfaces for anemones and their fish. The scenery consists of both soft and hard corals, massive boulder coral heads up to 5m across, and black coral trees. These are interspersed with encrusting and staghorn corals, gorgonian fans and a host of colourful soft corals. Observant divers can find queen murex, baler and spider shells, plus pincushion seastars, flatworms and an incredible variety of nudibranchs.

Tame fish-life abounds along the wall. Mackerel and trevally compete for your attention, along with more colourful reef fish such as butterflyfish, angelfish and clown triggerfish. Turtles are also seen on most dives.

15 HARDY REEF – FANTASEA DRIFT

Location: *Northwest corner inside channel*
Depth Range: *0-20m+ (0-66ft+)*
Access: *Fantasea Pontoon*
Expertise Rating: *Novice or intermediate*

Hardy Reef is a spectacular 13km-long reef with a suspended lagoon and three 'waterfalls' that drain it. There is an 80m-deep channel, with a few hundred metres between Hardy and its nearby reefs. Other sites provide enormous overhangs, rich fronts and tops, fascinating lagoons and edges of all sorts.

Diving from Reefworld, the Fantasea pontoon, is most comfortable. A flat decked tender (boat) from the pontoon

Snorkelers, semi-sub riders and divers all experience the great reef edges off the Whitsundays

The reeftop is flat with heavily grooved edges that give way to walls and overhangs falling down 10m to 30m, followed by a sand and rubble slope that drops away to 65m. The sealife is best above 20m and the underside of the pontoon is fantastic for macro and wide-angle close-up photography.

16	**KNUCKLE REEF – WALKING STICK**

Location: *Southwest corner of reef*
Depth Range: *0-40m+ (0-130ft)*
Access: *Boat*
Expertise Rating: *Novice (inside); advanced (outside)*

At this superb anchorage, the reef is shaped like, you guessed it, a walking stick. It's an easy site for snorkelers and divers as long as you watch your depth. Entry and exit locations will be determined by the ebbing or flooding of the tide.

Cruise Whitsunday has a Reef pontoon here. An easy drift dive takes you down a wall to 20m, where a slope quickly drops below 40m. At the base of the wall (at the stick 'handle'), there is an enormous overhang about 10m high and wide.

Shoaling fish hover along the wall, where fan corals reach out into the strong currents for plankton. Look for the resident hump-headed wrasse in the channel on the northern part of the site, along with passing mackerel and trout. These fish can be seen whether you're snorkeling or diving. Visibility ranges from 10m to 25m, averaging about 15m. Take your time, as the many smaller overhangs, nooks and crannies provide hideaways for cuttlefish and other cryptic critters.

Once inside the lagoon area there is a great snorkeling, night dive site and

safety stop area. At night, look for sea cucumbers and their commensal animals, and shells on the sandy floor.

17	**REEF 19-119 – JUST MAGIC**

Location: *Both sides of elongate reef*
Depth Range: *1-20m+ (3-66ft+)*
Access: *Boat only and usually parachute entries from a hot boat*
Expertise Rating: *Advanced*

An exciting drift dive when you can get to it, Just Magic lives up to its name. A parachute hot boat entry drops you in about 20m from the reef and you must swim straight in to the edge or risk being carried away when the tides are running.

Carry a safety sausage on this dive and listen to the divemaster's brief, as it is quite possible to wash off the end of the reef when you're finishing the dive. You may need to do a mid-water safety stop.

This is an almost linear, but small reef loaded with spectacular coral and fish life. You have the option to swim deep to 40m+, or stay shallower above 20m where the life is more interesting. Watch your depth constantly along this vertical wall, which juts to and fro on a 60-degree slope. The bottom is well beyond 40m. Nearer the surface, the wall has a right-angle shoulder to the reeftop, which exposes on very low tides.

This colourful site has almost 100% coral cover with spectacular formations, especially branching and table forms of the staghorn group.

The larger fish include passing mackerel, tuna, trevally and barracuda. Large numbers of blue pullers and other planktivores are all over and close to the coral – great for wide-angle photography.

*Lace coral provides a delicate
comparison to the soft fan coral*

Townsville & Magnetic Island Dive Sites

The Museum of Tropical Queensland houses the Pandora relics and nearby is Reef HQ and Omnimax Theatre at Townsville

The third largest city in Queensland, Townsville averages 300 days of sunshine a year, is home to the Museum of Tropical Queensland, Reef HQ Aquarium and Omnimax Theatre, Australian Institute of Marine Science, Great Barrier Reef Marine Park Authority (GBRMPA), regional centre for the EPA, Commonwealth Scientific and Industrial Research Organisation (CSIRO) and James Cook University. It is a fascinating city, widely recognised as the capital of North Queensland. It has a range of accommodation, dining and entertainment options, which you'll also find on Magnetic Island, a fun destination just a short ferry ride from town. With the island and rainforest-clad ranges surrounding Townsville, this truly tropical city has great options for all activities.

Townsville Reefs & Magnetic Island

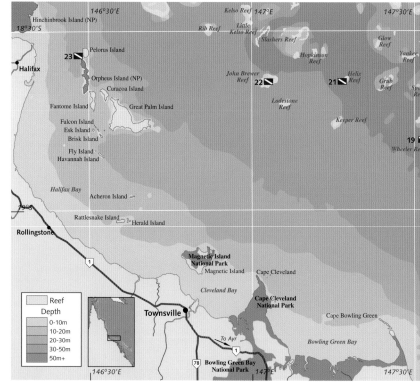

A variety of dive operators run from Townsville, servicing the *Yongala,* Coral Sea and nearby reefs. Three day cruises to Cairns are also available.

The Palm Islands to the north are mainland-type islands with good fringing reefs, much like Magnetic Island's, but better due to their greater length. Orpheus Island has a resort and James Cook University's Research Station. Still further north, Dunk, Hinchinbrook and Bedarra Islands have resorts serviced from Townsville, Cardwell and Mission Beach.

Reefs off Townsville are diverse and offer a great variety of diving. From here you can reach the *Yongala* and *Gothenberg* shipwrecks, plus others that remain unidentified. Some, like the Foam,

are protected and no entry is permitted. Townsville has a hyperbaric medicine unit and the only recompression chamber in Queensland, so if you're going to get bent, it's best to do it near here!

Townsville & Magnetic Island Dive Sites	GOOD SNORKELING	NOVICE	INTERMEDIATE	ADVANCED
18 YONGALA				•
19 WHEELER REEF		•	•	
20 DAVIES REEF		•	•	
21 HELIX REEF – HIGH VOLTAGE		•	•	
22 JOHN BREWER REEF		•	•	
23 PELORUS ISLAND		•	•	
24 FLINDERS REEF – CHINA WALL		•		•

0 ———— 30 km
0 ———— 20 miles
not for navigation

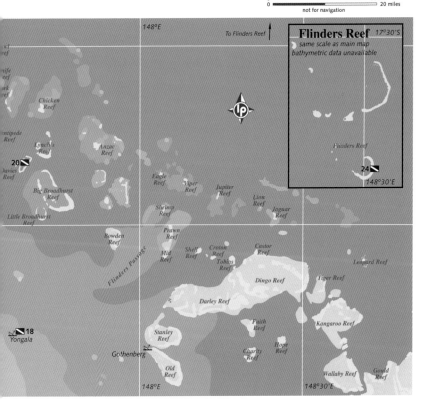

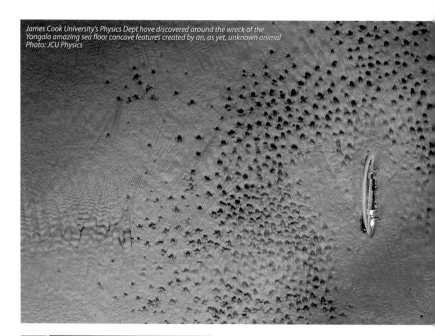

James Cook University's Physics Dept have discovered around the wreck of the Yongala amazing sea floor concave features created by an, as yet, unknown animal
Photo: JCU Physics

18 YONGALA

Location: *25 km (14 miles) east of Cape Bowling Green*
Depth Range: *15-33m (49-108ft)*
Access: *Boat*
Expertise Rating: *Advanced*

The *Yongala* is undoubtedly Queensland's best wreck dive. This passenger and general cargo steamer was lost in a cyclone in 1911 when she was headed to Cairns on her 99th run along the Queensland coast. The ship departed Mackay Harbour without telegraph equipment and was too far out before it could be warned of the oncoming cyclone. Details of the ship's sinking are unknown, but it was likely swamped by massive waves that left its 121 crew and passengers no way to escape.

The *Yongala* is a significant cultural site and is protected under both the GBR Marine Park regulations and the Commonwealth Government's Historic Shipwrecks Act (1976). Regulations prohibit any activity that is likely to damage the fabric of the wreck or unduly disturb the prolific (and spectacular) flora and fauna that has colonised the sunken hull. This includes prohibited activities such as fishing, removing artefacts and spearing fish.

Several dive shops offer tours to the wreck. Visitors on charter vessels will be briefed by the operator about the do's and don'ts of diving the site, while those on private vessels will need a permit to enter the protected zone around the wreck. The permit will list the conditions and code of conduct for diving on this and all historic wrecks off Queensland.

Access to this site is weather and permission dependent – tide runs and sea state can make this a hazardous dive. A giant stride from a moored boat down a buoyed descent line makes an exciting beginning to an incredibly interesting dive.

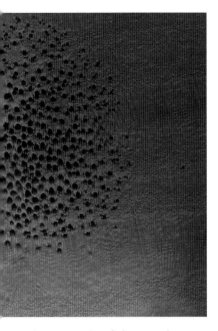

The port side of the vessel comes into view first and if the tidal current is running you can 'hide' in the lee of the hull and work your dive from there. As the entire hull is richly encrusted with soft and hard corals, hydroids, oysters, fan and whip gorgonians, it is a superb macro site. The cruising schools of kingfish, trevally, turrum and barracuda provide good wide-angle shots. Sea snakes are common, as are bull rays, eagle rays, turtles and enormous groper. One groper, usually found under the bow or stern, is called V-Dub, because it's as big as a Volkswagon!

Thousands of oysters line the interior and under the bow and stern of the wreck, leaving piles of dead shells on the bottom. The wreck features coral trout, stripeys, surgeonfish, fusiliers, lionfish, damsels and often clouds of baitfish.

This 110m-long marine grave is truly an oasis in a 'desert' of sand – it deserves its total protection. Some say this is the best wreck dive in the world.

19 WHEELER REEF

Location: *Southwest corner near anchorage & sandy area off cay*
Depth Range: *3-40m (10-130ft)*
Access: *Boat*
Expertise Rating: *Novice*

This small cay is the only one in the whole area. The sand slope falling away from the cay provides delightful sandy floor diving between rich coral heads and patches. There is excellent fish diversity, especially in the mid-depth areas, with schools of pelagics occasionally zooming by.

Drop into the shallows and follow your dive plan as it is easy to go deep into the coral ridges. Lucky divers will get to see whitetip reef sharks resting on the bottom and the rare appearance of a leopard shark, but only in the deeper places. It's protected as a national park, so we are seeing more and more of the larger reef species that are targeted by fishers. The trout and sweetlip are becoming bigger and more common with the occasional sighting of a beautiful barramundi cod.

Large bommies provide settling places for plate and staghorn coral colonies with great diversity of damsel, cardinal and parrotfish. Take your time here and enjoy the end of the dive in the white sandy floors of the shallows.

Rich coral slopes abound on reefs off Townsville

20 MAGNETIC ISLAND

Location: *Any one of the many sites around the island*
Depth Range: *0-25m (0-75ft)*
Access: *Boat or beach*
Expertise Rating: *Novice to advanced*

Magnetic Island has a diverse range of great sites, many of which you can access straight from the beach. Several old wreck remains can be seen and coral life has gradually got better as the silt from dredging has been reduced during the past few years. Many of the communities are veneer reefs where the corals live on a granite substrate. This means cyclones can wipe out large areas, as they can on any reef. When conditions are ideal at the island, it is a great place for fish, corals and macro dives.

Primary sites are Alma, Arthur, Florence, Geoffrey and Nelly Bays, with Orchard Rocks and Bremer Point offering those with access to a boat an exciting deep dive.

There are great spots for muck diving, and corals and fish abound with sandy-floor bays also providing night diving opportunities. Wherever you dive here, take your time and look out for the oc-

casional large bommie, swim-through canyons, rich plate coral and stag thickets, which provide great habitats for the smaller fish. Large schools of pelagics will be seen in the deeper waters. Trout, batfish, parrotfish, angelfish and boxfish will be seen. Nudibranchs and other cryptic creatures are commonly seen by the careful observer.

Fringing reef communities are recovering well after dredge spoils were dumped further away from Magnetic Island. Photo: Andy Lewis

Exploring Shipwrecks

Penetration by divers can accelerate a wreck's deterioration. Even minor and inadvertent diver contact can cause structural damage. Divers' bubbles can cause active corrosion of fragile iron structures and bulkheads, especially where protective sediments and marine growths are damaged or disturbed.

Remember too that shipwreck penetration is a skilled specialty that should only be attempted with proper training. Wrecks are often unstable; they can be silty, deep and disorienting. Use an experienced guide to view wreck artefacts and the amazing coral communities that grow on them.

Many ships in the GBR Province are protected historic sites where, among other things, penetration is illegal. Several of the most important wrecks have additional special regulations. Make inquiries at the Museum of Tropical Queensland (☎ (07) 47 260 600; www.mtq.qld.gov.au; 84 Flinders St, Townsville)

Reefs off Townsville are some of the most studied in the world

Aggregations of fish are becoming more common in protected areas

21 | HELIX REEF – HIGH VOLTAGE

Location: *Southwest corner near anchorage & lagoon area*
Depth Range: *5-36m (16-118ft)*
Access: *Boat*
Expertise Rating: *Novice*

Helix has numerous good sites. The North Wall is an excellent drift dive for advanced divers. It is chock-full of great life, gullies and overhangs. High Voltage is excellent for all levels, as it has a sandy floor, plenty of depth ranges and an incredible array of swim-throughs and caves that form mazes of coral passageways.

Entry takes you down to about 20m, but you can easily swim to one of the nearby bommies. On your left, about five bommies have a network of swim-throughs between them. Most are open to the top, so light is good and they are generally safe. As you proceed, try to avoid fin, hose and gauge damage to the corals. One swim-through cave tracks from 16m in a spiral and exits at 6m. As you exit each swim-through you come into a vista of beautiful staghorn thickets and many types of fish.

Large giant clams are well spaced around the site and are as varied in colour as the fish. Damsels, butterflyfish, fusiliers, soldierfish, trout and cod are common with parrotfish and wrasse adding a rainbow of colour.

If you tire of the beauty of the bommies and mazes, then cross the staghorn thickets toward the reef. On your right, you'll come across Broken Bommie. This leads you to the reef edge and another swim-through between the reef and bommie. From here you can continue along the edge of the reef that surrounds a sandy lagoon area, and then back to the boat.

Feathery stinging hydroids should always be avoided

soft corals provide rich splashes of colour among the pastels of the hard plate and boulder corals.

Photo opportunities abound with the conditions of the day determining whether you go wide or close-up as the rougher conditions can lower the visibility. Look for clams, soft corals and clouds of blue pullers and passing trout or trevally to photograph. Bumpheaded parrotfish are often seen, as well as species of algae-eating parrotfish and wrasse.

Passing pelagics out near the edge areas will include mackerel, barracuda and tuna if you are lucky.

23 PELORUS ISLAND

Location: *Southwest side of northernmost Palm Island*
Depth Range: *1-15m (3-49ft)*
Access: *Boat/Beach*
Expertise Rating: *Novice*

22 JOHN BREWER REEF

Location: *Southwest corner near anchorages*
Depth Range: *5-38m (16-125ft)*
Access: *Boat*
Expertise Rating: *Novice*

Pelorus Island is the northern-most of the Palm Islands, a group of mainland islands boasting a mixture of habitats. They combine sandy and muddy beaches and bottoms, rich fringing reefs, mangroves and rocky shores. Many of the fringing reefs have excellent diving.

Accessing the Pelorus site is easy – fall off the Coral Princess pontoon into about 3m and then dive to your plan, either up-current, drifting back to the pontoon, or setting up a drift-and-dinghy pickup.

Snorkelers can enjoy the excellent fringing reef, nearby white sandy beach and, visibility willing, great viewing all round.

An established feeding station has been set up here at 5m, so the fish are tame and usually impatiently waiting for divers. Sergeant majors, monocle bream, moon wrasse, rabbitfish, red em-

John Brewer is a rich reef today, but was devastated by crown-of-thorns seastars in the late 1960s and again in the 1980s, showing how a reef can recover quite well. Occasional crown-of-thorns can still be seen, leaving their white feeding scars where they have eaten the living coral off its limestone skeleton. There are numerous dive sites to be found suiting the novice through to advanced diver with shallow lagoon-like dives and then deeper dives off the walls and back reef bommies. Colourful

peror, harlequin tuskfish and the occasional moray eel all gather for the feed.

After the feeding frenzy, follow the slope along the reef edge. This fringing reef is rich due to the mud, sand, current and depths. You can travel anywhere from 5m to 15m and have a great dive. A diversity of corals – soft, gorgonian, fan, whip, hard, mushroom and stinging – are present here.

Bull, eagle and Kuhl's rays can often be seen cruising around or resting on the bottom.

Pelagics are here but usually hard to see in the lower visibility. Beware the stinging hydroids, which look deceptively tame with their beautiful white feathers or delicate brown/white hard colonies – they deliver a painful sting when touched.

Pelorus Island has a superb beach and dive site
Photo: www.coralprincess.com.au

Fragile white lace coral is always a macro-photographer's delight

24 | FLINDERS REEF – CHINA WALL

Location: *Eastern wall of reef*
Depth Range: *1-40m+ (10-130ft+)*
Access: *Boat*
Expertise Rating: *Intermediate*

Flinders Reef is an atoll about 37km-long and 28km-wide. It has a cay and weather tower and represents Coral Sea diving at its best. China Wall is one of the best dives on Flinders, Dart, Abington and Shark reefs, although each has its own unique features. On most of these reefs, the walls drop away to over 305m (1000ft)

Good fish diversity occurs in the shallows with emperor angelfish, clown triggerfish and schools of goatfish feeding on the sand. Bump-headed parrotfish are regularly seen with pelagic surgeons, dogtooth tuna, trevally and barracuda. The prowlers include silvertip, grey whaler and whitetip reef sharks. On a good day you will also see lionfish and Pavo razorfish, which hover vertically by the staghorn coral.

Hard corals are small, slow-growing and found in more protected grooves or on the reeftop. You will see staghorns and tabulates in addition to golf ball and brain type corals. Stinging corals are common, with their light brownish-to-white colonies growing in bizarre shapes. Softs and gorgonians are also present.

Many critters can be found in the wall's crevices and overhangs, especially lace corals, sponges, small clams, nudibranchs, morays, anemones and feather stars. Night diving brings out more crabs, shrimps and enormous basket stars.

Caves, caverns and swim-throughs are all along these walls, just waiting to be explored. Sometimes manta rays and hammerhead sharks appear, along with schooling hammerheads deep in the colder water during winter. You may be lucky enough to see billfish here as well.

Shoaling pelagics are common Coral Sea sights

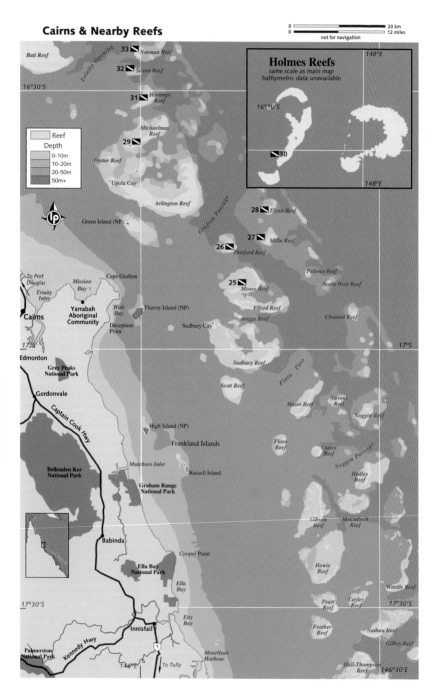

Cairns & Nearby Reefs

0 _____ 20 km
0 _____ 12 miles
not for navigation

Batt Reef

33 Norman Reef

Trinity Opening

32 Saxon Reef

16°30'S

31 Hastings Reef

Michaelmas Reef

29

Oyster Reef

Upolu Cay

Arlington Reef

Grafton Passage

28 Flynn Reef

Green Island (NP)

27 Milln Reef

26 Thetford Reef

Pellowe Reef

To Port Douglas

Mission Bay

Cape Grafton

North West Reef

Trinity Inlet

25 Moore Reef

Cairns

Yarrabah Aboriginal Community

Wide Bay

Fitzroy Island (NP)

Elford Reef

Briggs Reef

Channel Reef

Deception Point

Sudbury Cay

17°S

Edmonton

Grey Peaks National Park

Sudbury Reef

Flora Pass

Gordonvale

Scott Reef

Captain Cook Hwy

Maori Reef

Stevens Reef

Noggin Reef

High Island (NP)

Frankland Islands

Flora Reef

Noggin Passage

Bellenden Ker National Park

Mutchero Inlet

Russell Island

Coates Reef

Hedley Reef

Graham Range National Park

Babinda

Cooper Point

Gibson Reef

McCulloch Reef

Ella Bay National Park

Ella Bay

Howie Reef

Wardle Reef

17°30'S

Peart Reef

Cayley Reef

17°30'S

Etty Bay

Innisfail

Feather Reef

Nathan Reef

Palmerston National Park

Kennedy Hwy

Mourilyan Harbour

Gilbey Reef

146°E

To Tully

Hall-Thompson Reef

146°30'E

Reef
Depth
- 0-10m
- 10-20m
- 20-50m
- 50m+

Holmes Reefs
same scale as main map
bathymetric data unavailable

148°E

16°30'S

30

148°E

Cairns & Nearby Reefs Dive Sites

Inquisitive fish seem to follow divers at many locations

A true tourism centre with many nearby reef, rainforest and outback facilities, Cairns allows those with a shorter timeframe to 'do it all' from one convenient location. Truly a tropical city, it has everything a visitor could ask for: warm climate, amazing rainforest-clad mountain ranges, an excellent range of accommodation, dining establishments, shopping, a casino, and many tour operations.

The nearby rainforest-clad Great Dividing Range makes an excellent backdrop to this harbour city and region with a population of more than 120,000. Whitewater rafting, fishing, calm-water mangrove cruises, bungee jumping, parachuting, rainforest tours, helicopter flights, diving day-trips, extended trips or charters are all there for the asking.

The diving and snorkeling options from Cairns is impressive. If you have limited time, it's best to book before you leave home as it can sometimes be difficult to get the trip you want. With more time to spare, you'll have the opportunity to shop around for the trip – and weather – that suits your needs.

Reefs and islands just offshore are excellent. Green Island is a developed tourist spot on a coral cay, with good snorkeling and diving, serviced by several operators. Fitzroy Island is a mainland island with good fringing reefs. Other islands here are for day visits only, with Michaelmas Cay being an internationally significant bird rookery.

Reefs off Innisfail, to the south, are quite different to those off Cairns and Port Douglas, to the north (the start of the Ribbon Reefs). Innisfail reefs tend to be broken into isolated coral patches, while the reefs off Cairns become more solid and the Ribbons are elongated shelf-edge shapes. Diving or snorkeling on all of them is fantastic.

Trips from Cairns access the Coral Sea, far northern reefs and from Port Douglas to Lizard Island. Some operators allow you to go out on their day boat and then stay overnight on the reef on a 'mother ship,' which may move daily from reef-to-reef. Amphibious aircraft and helicopter options are also available.

Cairns & Nearby Reefs Dive Sites	GOOD SNORKELING	NOVICE	INTERMEDIATE	ADVANCED
25 MOORE REEF	•	•		
26 THETFORD REEF	•		•	
27 MILLN REEF – THREE SISTERS	•		•	
28 FLYNN REEF – CORAL GARDENS	•	•		
29 MICHAELMAS REEF	•	•		
30 HOLMES REEF – AMAZING	•		•	
31 HASTINGS REEF – THE FISH BOWL	•	•		
32 SAXON REEF	•	•		
33 NORMAN REEF – TROPPO LOUNGE	•	•		

Rich back reef communities grade onto white sand slopes on many northern reefs

25 MOORE REEF

Location: *Sunlover Cruises mooring*
Depth Range: *1-25m (3-82ft)*
Access: *Boat*
Expertise Rating: *Novice or Advanced*

Several operators run trips out to Moore Reef, a site rich with marine life. Operators work the back reef areas, all of which have similar dives.

Each dive takes you over staghorn thickets on sand that slopes out and drops to 22m. You can go out right or left to the bommies, or closer in to the reef edge. Some bommies have great swim-throughs and the smaller ones in-between are also well worth exploring. As you swim out, watch for rays buried in the sand.

Bommies and gullies in the reef side make excellent sites for fish observation. The larger bommies usually come to within a few metres of the surface, so you can dive at whatever depth you feel most comfortable. At night you'll see nudibranchs, crabs, worms and outstretched coral polyps. Also look for occasional crayfish.

The abundant hard coral is in good condition, interspersed with soft coral hiding grounds for damselfish, which dash out to catch planktonic food. Wrasse are common, along with parrotfish, emperors, butterflyfish and surgeonfish.

A school of grey reef sharks has been spotted here, but you're more likely to see a whitetip reef shark resting on the sand. This site probably suits macro-photography best – especially at night – but you can also get the odd wide-angle shot.

butterflyfish, rabbitfish, damsels, angelfish and the occasional pipefish. Moving over to the bommies, you'll be confronted with many swim-throughs. Most are partially closed on top, sending magical shafts of light down into these mysterious passageways.

The large gorgonian fans and soft corals that occur in these tunnels need special care, so watch your fins. Anemones are common, with several species of commensal fish and beautiful transparent shrimps cavorting within their tentacles. As always, it is the slow and observant diver who will get to see them.

Some of the boulder coral heads have dozens of multi-colored Christmas tree worms. The bright whorls of their brachial plumes make them look like little pairs of their namesake. These whorls are used for feeding and breathing. If you get too close, the polychaete worm will retract back into its tube in the coral, pulling a cap over the end for protection.

A fish-feeding permit allows the Coral Princess to attract trevally, wrasse, spangled emperor, red bass, blue-and-gold fusiliers and sergeant majors for the benefit of guests.

26   THETFORD REEF

Location: *Bommie fields, northwest side of reef*
Depth Range: *1-25m (3-82ft)*
Access: *Boat*
Expertise Rating: *Intermediate*

Almost 2km-long with scattered coral heads along its back (leeward) edge, Thetford provides numerous dive sites to choose from. Be careful of your navigation and take along a safety sausage, as it is easy to find yourself disoriented well away from the boat with no dive time left.

Sandy floors between the numerous coral bommies are covered with smaller coral patches and blue staghorn thickets. Look among these for giant clams,

Blue-lined angelfish are shy and hard to photograph

27 MILLN REEF – THREE SISTERS

Location: *NW Milln Reef – moorings*
Depth Range: *1-33m (3-108ft)*
Access: *Boat*
Expertise Rating: *Intermediate*

Outer reefs are hammered by regular rough seas

The Three Sisters are a series of three large bommies lined up at the back of the reef, with the sites of Whale Bommie, the Desert, Petaj Mooring and Swimming Pools nearby. The deepest sister rises from about 33m off sand on the northwestern side, coming to within 1m of the surface. Closer to the reef on an easterly bearing, the other two sisters are shallower, with the innermost bommie in about 14m off a sand-and-rubble bottom.

If there is little current, ideally start your first dive on the deepest bommie, which has steep sides and may have schools of fusiliers, various snappers and chub. As you head down the walls, you'll see barracuda hanging silently in the blue. At the bottom, coral trout and cod move in and out of overhangs and crevices. A superb stand of black coral on the bommies' deepest side is home to commensal gobies.

In good visibility, you may be able to see the second sister, about 40m to the east. After spiraling up the first large bommie, head to the east. You will likely see several whitetip sharks resting on the sand. They will lazily swim away if you approach, only to return to the same place a few minutes later.

A green turtle has made Three Sisters its favourite haunt, and is often seen lying motionless near the surface around the second sister, where it feeds on sponges and algae. The depth at the second sister is about 19m, making it ideal for exploring around the base, where you are likely to see more sharks, blue-spotted rays and other sand dwellers.

After circling the bommie and upon approaching the third sister, you'll be confronted by a memorable sight. The walls between sister two and three are straight-sided and only about 3m apart, and are often crammed with schools of fusiliers and snapper. If this weren't enough, brilliant gold or yellow gorgonians jut out from the walls like impenetrable curtains – a spectacular photographic opportunity for a wide-angle lens.

On your way back, a swim-through on the north side of the first sister is safe and exits to more shallow bommies where abundant fish and coral can make your safety stop interesting. Alternatively, keep swimming to the wall on the edge of the back reef to finish off in the shallows.

Green turtles will be seen by lucky divers

Clam species come in three sizes: small, medium and giant

28 FLYNN REEF – CORAL GARDENS

Location: *NW Flynn Reef – moorings*
Depth Range: *1-27m (3-89ft)*
Access: *Boat*
Expertise Rating: *Novice*

Flynn Reef has several well known dive sites, including Gordon's Mooring, Tennis Court and Tracy's Bommie, which supply good bommie swim-throughs, walls, overhangs, crevices and night diving. The Coral Gardens mooring sits in 8m on a sandy bottom. In front is a wall from 5m to the surface, along the reef edge.

Extending back from the wall are superb coral gardens, complete with stands of staghorn coral among terraces of table corals, boulder coral heads and plates, with swaying soft corals in between. You need to practice your no-touch diving here, as the many small critters will test your identification skills to the limit. Dropping away from this plateau of coral is a terracing slope down 10m to 20m.

This slope is richly covered in coral stands and giant clams. Down deeper there are fan corals and even more staghorn thickets on the sand, with occasional good trevally and mackerel pelagic action. Clownfish, batfish, trout, cod, fusiliers, butterflyfish and angelfish, basslets and whitetip reef sharks are some of the frequent visitors. Lucky divers may see grey reef sharks and octopus, along with more common moray eels, barracuda, lionfish and nudibranchs.

There are numerous opportunities for a safety stop on your way out of this site as well.

29 | MICHAELMAS REEF

Location: *Northwest reef back*
Depth Range: *1-20m (3-66ft)*
Access: *Boat*
Expertise Rating: *Novice*

Michaelmas Reef is 10km (6 miles) long with a sand cay – an important rookery for sooty and crested terns. It has enormous potential for diving. This site description is an amalgamation of many sites here, but is demonstrative of most dives available.

Giant clams are the most common and delightful feature of this reef. You will see them whether snorkeling the shallows or diving to 20m, although they are more prolific in shallower areas. Also look for soft corals with hard bases that contribute to reef growth throughout this area.

Walls, swim-throughs, gullies, small caves and overhangs are found in most areas and are often homes to whitetip reef sharks. Snorkeling takes you over shallow reeftops riddled with holes, crevices and many giant clams. Smaller burrowing clams are common and tend to be more iridescent and varied in colour. Blue-spotted rays and sea cucumbers are common on the sandy floors, with schools of damsels and fusiliers all over the corals.

If you dive or snorkel near the beach of the cay, you'll have the disconcerting experience of fish, and sometimes even small sharks, dashing in and 'biting' at your heels as you walk on the sand. Fear not! They are merely trying to catch the shrimp and other animals lifted from out of the sand as you walk, having learned that humans are useful for something. The faster or more vigorously you move the more excited they will become, as you stir up more food for them!

As you explore the bommies, you'll encounter batfish, cleaner stations, nudibranchs, crayfish, turtle weed clumps and a constantly changing parade of life.

On lucky days you may see the cowtail ray, eagle ray, or schools of pelagics cruising by in deeper water. Anemones are scattered all over, thickets of blue and brown staghorn corals adding colour to all activities.

30 | HOLMES REEF – AMAZING

Location: *Holmes Reef*
Depth Range: *5-40m+ (16-130ft+)*
Access: *Moored boat only*
Expertise Rating: *Intermediate*

From the sheer walls and pinnacles, swim-throughs and sandy floors to the abundant life throughout the whole area, this site is truly amazing in its appearance from the surface and as you dive it. There are many dive sites on each of these Coral Sea reefs with elements of Amazing, often with great pelagic action in clear waters.

If the whitetip reef sharks haven't overly distracted you as you descend, you may see thousands of tiny 'umbrella handles' sticking out of the sand, seemingly dancing and disappearing as you approach. Take your time and approach slowly; you'll seldom get closer than about 4m before they vanish into their burrows.

Minifin parrotfish often have food algae growing on their fused teeth

Wrasse will often move coral rubble about looking for food

Down the slope at 35m are two large coral outcrops called The Matterhorn, resembling mountains protruding from snow. These have glorious sea fans, soft corals, fairy basslets and cruising grey reef sharks. Be careful of your depth here as it drops away to 60m and into the abyss.

Back up the slope, the reef starts at 25m and rises quickly to 10m. This wall is where awesome swim-throughs can be found. On a sunny day they have a laser show of sunbeams streaking through the holes above, so you don't need a torch for daytime entries. Watch for several resident potato cod and spotted sweetlip schools. Banded coral shrimp also give themselves away with their long white antennae poking out of crevices.

As you finish your dive with a safety stop at the top of the mooring pinnacle, entertainment is often provided by clownfish, passing bluespot trevally and occasionally giant trevally.

Night diving here is easy due to the shallows and complex of gullies and swim-throughs. If you face your torch toward yourself (so the beam is hidden), you'll see a spectacular display of flashlight fish.

along the wall it is possible to go left out to a series of bommies).

Anemones and clumps of staghorn coral are regular features, with giant clams perched in the shallows on the reeftop and bommies. Sweetlip, cod and trout are regulars and schools of damsels are common. Pairs of butterflyfish and angelfish feeding among the coral add more splashes of colour. The wall winds around and along, bringing you to more clams and a good swim-through up into the reef. After exploring here, go left around the group of bommies. Note also the giant clam on the outer edge's base in 12m.

By making your way back along the wall, you can return the way you came or take a different depth or route out over the floor. Whitetip reef sharks and lagoon rays are often seen, along with less common turtles.

On some of the coral patches you will see long white tentacles extending out over the sand. These are the feeding threads of a Terrebellid worm and if you get close enough to the ribbon-like tentacles, you will see lumps of food being carried along inside them. Also notice the daytime coral, with polyps out about 6cm to 10cm. You will often find broken off satellite pieces establishing new colonies.

31	**HASTINGS REEF – THE FISH BOWL**

Location: *Mooring*
Depth Range: *0-16m (0-53ft)*
Access: *Boat*
Expertise Rating: *Novice*

Hastings is a large, popular diving and snorkeling reef, with over 13km of reef edge and back reef sand floors to explore. Upon entering the water at The Fish Bowl, head to the wall that runs along the reef's back edge and drops to a sandy floor at 8m to 12m (as you move

Maori wrasse are becoming more regularly seen in protected areas

32 SAXON REEF

Location: *Moorings*
Depth Range: *1-20m (3-66ft)*
Access: *Boat*
Expertise Rating: *Novice*

Another popular location used by several operators, this is an excellent back reef offering several night or day dive sites combined here into one 'mega site.' Snorkeling anywhere on the shallow bommie tops, reef edge and reeftop here is excellent.

The reeftop is exposed on low tides, with a wall dropping down 8m onto a white sand floor. Moving out from the wall, large patches of staghorn coral thickets and small bommies are interspersed with large single-species and mixed-species bommies. Swim-throughs and gullies are scattered throughout the area. Your guide can help you find the best sites to explore.

There is no need to go below 18m, as the rubble sand and few coral patches beyond pale into insignificance compared with the life further up the slope. Each bommie has its own special feature and life associated with it – giant clams, anemones, corallimorpharians, pipefish, lionfish and moray eels. Occasionally a turtle may cruise by, as can large cod and ever-present schools of damsels and fusiliers. Passing pelagics are common and include tuna, mackerel, trevally and barracuda.

The white sandy floor always lifts the light and on a sunny day transforms the whole area into a classic, magical reef scene. Wide-angle photography and macro work well here, but watch the sand glare effect. Giant clams make great subjects but watch nesting titan triggerfish in summer, as they protect their 'bomb crater' nests with crash-tackling effectiveness.

A pair of anemone fish hover over their eggs exposed by a careless diver

33 NORMAN REEF – TROPPO LOUNGE

Location: *Moorings*
Depth Range: *0-27m (0-89ft)*
Access: *Boat*
Expertise Rating: *Novice*

This superb little reef has moorings belonging to several dive operations, with each using different areas of the reef's back.

Maori wrasse, moray eels, giant clams, anemones and their commensals are all permanent features. Along the reef back are a series of large bommies, staghorn

thickets and hillocks of rich coral cover. Sandy areas deeper down often have garden eels but you may need to wait for them to emerge, as they are very timid.

Almost all dives start with a giant stride entry from the boat. Depending on your experience, you either swim up to the shallows or out deeper and then back in. Amphitheatre-like sandy floors are surrounded by coral hillocks, reef edge and bommies. Take your time around the bommies and at the reef edge, as there are some excellent swim-throughs and a few caves, some of which are not safe for divers – you will need a guide to show and lead the way. Walls of all sizes and shapes with gullies, crevices and overhangs are common.

In mid-to-late winter, minke whales can be present in this whole area of reefs. Batfish, drummers, spangled emperors, fusiliers and red bass are common. Several large resident Maori wrasse will join you on your dive, especially if you ignore them. When you pay them any specific attention, they tend to shy away.

Turtles are regulars, but tend to leave as soon as you see them. Moray eels can also be found throughout the area, with blue-spotted rays and giant clams common on the sandy floor.

Wide-angle and macrophotography are both rewarding here, with the occasional whitetip shark adding a thrill if you get the shot.

Port Douglas

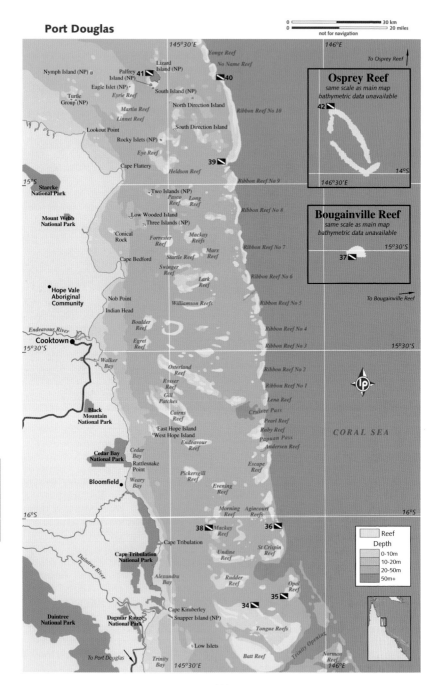

0 —————————— 30 km
0 —————————— 20 miles
not for navigation

145°30'E   146°E

To Osprey Reef

Yonge Reef
No Name Reef
Lizard Island (NP)
Nymph Island (NP)   Palfrey   41
Island (NP)
Eagle Islet (NP)   South Island (NP)   40
Turtle   Eyrie Reef
Group (NP)
Martin Reef   North Direction Island
Linnet Reef   Ribbon Reef No 10
Lookout Point
South Direction Island
Rocky Islets (NP)
Eye Reef
Cape Flattery   39
Heldson Reef

Osprey Reef
same scale as main map
bathymetric data unavailable
42

14°S
146°30'E

15°S
Starcke
National Park   Ribbon Reef No 9

Two Islands (NP)
Pasco   Long
Reef   Reef
Mount Webb   Low Wooded Island   Ribbon Reef No 8
National Park   Three Islands (NP)

Bougainville Reef
same scale as main map
bathymetric data unavailable

Conical   Mackay
Rock   Forrester   Reefs   15°30'S
Reef
Cape Bedford   Marx   Ribbon Reef No 7
Startle Reef   Reef   37
Swinger
Reef
Lark
Reef   Ribbon Reef No 6

Hope Vale   Nob Point   Williamson Reefs   Ribbon Reef No 5
Aboriginal
Community   To Bougainville Reef
Indian Head
Boulder
Reef   Ribbon Reef No 4
Endeavour River   Egret   Ribbon Reef No 3   15°30'S
Cooktown   Reef
15°30'S
Walker   Osterland   Ribbon Reef No 2
Bay   Reef
Rosser   Ribbon Reef No 1
Reef   LP
Gill
Patches   Lena Reef
Black   Cairns   Cruiser Pass
Mountain   Reef   Pearl Reef
National Park   East Hope Island   Ruby Reef   CORAL SEA
West Hope Island   Papuan Pass
Endeavour   Andersen Reef
Cedar Bay   Cedar   Reef
National Park   Bay   Escape
Rattlesnake   Reef
Point
Bloomfield   Weary   Pickersgill
Bay   Reef
Evening
Reef
16°S   Morning   Agincourt   16°S
Reef   Reefs
38   Mackay   36
Reef
Cape Tribulation   Reef   Reef   0-10m
Cape Tribulation   Undine   St Crispin   Depth
National Park   Reef   Reef   10-20m
20-50m
Alexandra   Rudder   50m+
Daintree River   Bay   Reef   Opal
Reef
35
Cape Kimberley
34
Daintree   Dagmar Range   Snapper Island (NP)
National Park   National Park
Tongue Reefs
Low Islets
To Port Douglas   Trinity   Batt Reef   Norman
Bay   145°30'E   Reef
146°E

Reef
Depth
0-10m
10-20m
20-50m
50m+

Port Douglas Dive Sites

A catamaran makes a fast exit from the Port Douglas headlands
Photo: Richard l'Anson

A famed 'hideaway' for movie stars and presidents, Port Douglas is Australia's premier tropical destination. No longer a sleepy village, it is decidedly friendly, casual and energetic, with the highest number of restaurants per capita in the country.

Port (as it is locally known) is the coastal centre located closest to the Australian Wet Tropics (which includes 19 National Parks, 31 State Forests, timber reserves and an Aboriginal Reserve) and the Great Barrier Reef (GBR). Both of these enormous areas were designated UNESCO World Heritage Areas, in 1988 and 1981 respectively.

Port's Four Mile beach is delightful, with a central marina harbouring many dive boats, yachts and private vessels. Adventure trips in addition to diving and snorkeling include rafting, kayaking, horse riding, ballooning, 4WD, motorcycling and mountain biking. A wide range of accommodations – from camping grounds to 5-star hotels – are available.

Day trips to the reefs (starting around 90 minutes) can be made on large wave-piercing catamarans, smaller 10-30 person vessels and helicopters. Several extended stay and charter boats operate to the Ribbon Reefs, Coral Sea and Far Northern Reefs from here as well. Low Isles, just 15km offshore, is a popular nearby destination, with a sand cay and mangrove cay on a typical mid-shelf reef. The mangrove cay is closed during the nesting season of thousands of Torresian Imperial Pigeons, from August to February. Agincourt and Opal Reefs extend southwards from the Ribbons and are also popular outer edge reefs on this narrow part of the continental shelf, generally giving better visibility.

Port Douglas Dive Sites

	GOOD SNORKELING	NOVICE	INTERMEDIATE	ADVANCED
34 TONGUE REEF – TURTLE BAY	●	●		
35 OPAL REEF – BARRACUDA PASS	●		●	
36 AGINCOURT REEF – CASTLE ROCK	●	●		
37 THE ZOO – BOUGANVILLE REEF	●	●		
38 MACKAY REEF	●	●		
39 PIXIE'S PINNACLE	●	●		
40 RIBBON REEF NO 10 – THE COD HOLE	●	●		
41 LIZARD ISLAND – COBIA HOLE			●	
42 OSPREY REEF – NORTH HORN	●		●	

34 TONGUE REEF – TURTLE BAY

Location: *North end Third Sister Reef in Tongue Complex*
Depth Range: *1-15m (3-49ft)*
Access: *Boat*
Expertise Rating: *Novice*

A giant stride entry will often put you face-to-face with 'Killer', a 35kg Maori wrasse. You'll find the reef edge in about 3m – watch for one of several resident turtles often seen here. If you are lucky, 'Dopey', identified by his quiet nature and a nick in his back right flipper, will swim right into your view finder.

Working around the circle of reef will take you over one enormous giant clam and several species of sea cucumbers, on the sandy floor of this back reef cove. A staghorn thicket and patches provide hiding places for many smaller reef fish, which are also tucked along the small walls and bommies you pass.

A good mixture of soft and hard corals cover the reef edges and small bommies. Check under the plate corals for hovering trout, sweetlip and the occasional barramundi cod.

Finish the dive in the shallows adjacent to the reef edge. It is an easy swim back to the boat – the bottom can be interesting for those willing to look hard for smaller, more cryptic life.

Black-spotted toadfish could bite the end off a teasing finger

35 OPAL REEF – BARRACUDA PASS

Location: *Between south and main Opal Reefs, Poseidon & Haba moorings*
Depth Range: *1-15m (3-49ft)*
Access: *Boat*
Expertise Rating: *Intermediate*

Port Douglas dive boat operators love North and South Opal Reefs for the numerous great dive sites, including Bashful Bommie, Ayer's Rock, SNO, Cathedrals, Split Bommie, Blue Buoy, and One Fin Bommie. At Barracuda Point your entry drops you into a sandbox in 6m, which leads the way

Flame angelfish are surprisingly bright when seen underwater
Photo: Phil Woodhead

to a line of small bommies connected by beautiful coral gardens and sandy floors.

You can also start outside the pass for a drift dive. Either way, use the reef edge for navigation and watch your buddy and guide for a safe return. The tides bring lots of plankton through this opening, attracting smaller fish, which in turn attract bigger fish, thereby attracting bigger fish, and so on.

Note the bottom here, as the size of the sand grains gives an idea of how rugged it can get around reefs. Sea cucumbers abound on the sand – look at them carefully for commensals, if you can tear your eyes away from the superb soft and hard corals and grazing fish. You may see the occasional lagoon ray in the sand as well. The water deepens to your left as the fish life increases on your right. Schools of paddletail, trevally, mackerel, red bass and three species of barracuda move around slowly. A resident blacktip reef shark may also show itself.

This underwater 'rolling hills and valleys' area of coral is interspersed with sand. The nursery plate, three plate corals about 40cm off the sand, has provided shelter for a succession of juvenile whitetip reef sharks, which can usually be found at this site. The occasional giant clam can also be seen here, as well as titan triggerfish – which can get very aggressive in summer – digging their crater-shaped nests.

This is a superb site in most conditions and always great for photography, both wide-angle and macro.

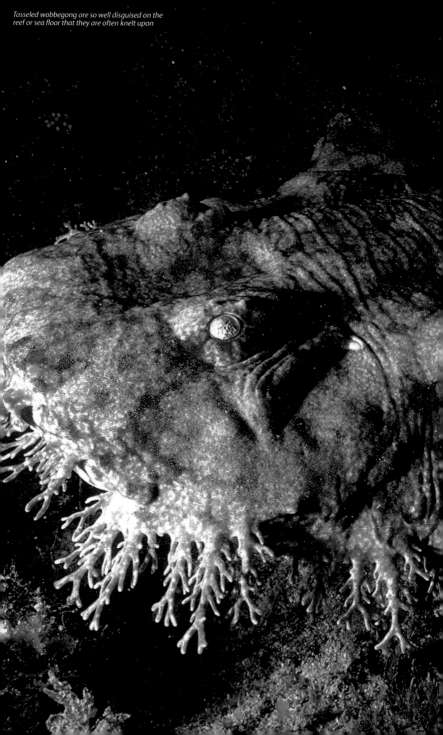

Tasseled wobbegong are so well disguised on the reef or sea floor that they are often knelt upon

36 AGINCOURT REEF – CASTLE ROCK

Location: *Southern end Agincourt Reef*
Depth Range: *0-25m (0-77ft)*
Access: *Boat*
Expertise Rating: *Novice – Intermediate*

Agincourt Reef is a complex of many smaller reefs, with snorkel sites at the pontoons and more than 20 excellent dive sites including Point Break, Phil's, Barracuda Bommie, Three Sisters, Horseshoe Reef and the Fish Bowl.

The northern Agincourts are also used by day operators from Port Douglas. Pieces of a Taiwanese wreck feature at The Wreck, giant clams are found at all sites, as are resident Maori wrasse. Drifts, walls, swim-throughs, pinnacles, big fish and turtles, coral gardens and garden eels are also found in the area.

Castle Rock is a large rich coral pinnacle rising from a steep sand slope located at the southern end of Agincourt Reef. Just around the corner is the continental shelf drop-off into the 2000m Queensland Trench, with oceanic waters usually giving great visibility. This Castle Rock is a classic back-reef pinnacle providing superb deep and shallow dives. By circumnavigating the pinnacle you will see a great diversity of life in the water and on the sandy floor and pinnacle. Many other species of coral have settled onto the boulder coral, which provides the basis of this pinnacle, making numerous habitats for thousands of animals and plants. This is a great macro or wide-angle site.

'Axle' is a friendly 1.2m malabar groper who will interact with divers by swimming up and looking to be patted. Please don't however, as chemicals from sunscreen and your skin may be harmful. Curious triggerfish are common and an abundance of blue-lined yellow snappers and sergeant-major damselfish will be seen. Graceful blue-spotted lagoon rays can also be seen swimming or buried in the sand with only their eyes and tails showing, with the occasional white-tip reef shark resting nearby.

Christmas tree worms are to be found extended from the tubes they create within the boulder coral. Lionfish often lurk in branching corals or small overhangs, waiting to rush out and suck up passing prey. 'Daisy' the flowery cod may also make an appearance if she's in the area.

The reef shallows near the pinnacle are perfect for snorkelers and as a safety stop. Giant clams can be seen, along with lizardfish, parrotfish, wrasse, damselfish and rays. As the small plankton feeding blue-green chromis are approached, they will dart back into the staghorn corals for protection.

Soldierfish are night-time feeders seen hiding under overhangs by day
Photo: John Barnett

Adapting to pressures from surge and waves is the reeftop stubby coral

37 | THE ZOO – BOUGANVILLE REEF

Location: *Anchored boat*
Depth Range: *5-40m+ (16-130ft)*
Access: *Boat*
Expertise Rating: *Novice – Advanced*

One of the smaller Coral Sea Reefs, Bouganville has a delightful array of dive sites, ranging from moorings to drifts. The Sticks and Between Wrecks are great drifts, while Deep Six, Dungeons & Dragons, West Point, The Junkyard and Corner Shop are all accessed from moorings or hot boats. These sites present a challenge for photographers, due to the diversity of life that can be seen here – your biggest dilemma will be whether to take your wide-angle or macro lens. Good luck with your decision! (Hint: on a clear day, go wide.)

At The Zoo, follow the mooring line down onto the large coral bommie then go to either the coral sand gully or onto the outside wall. Either direction makes for a rewarding dive.

The sand gully slopes down from 14 to 30m and is usually a resting place for whitetip reef sharks and sometimes a black cowtail ray. The edges of the gully supply rich surfaces of coral, algae and coralline algae, all great spots to find nudibranchs, flatworms and leopard blennies.

Leading away from the edges of the gully and the shallows of the wall, numerous channels form a labyrinth. Each channel has swim-throughs and provides all sorts of shady and protected spots, with an array of fish life that will keep you busy identifying for a while. Surgeonfish, snappers, sweetlips, drummers and grazers are some of the larger species, while numerous smaller species reward the careful observer.

On the outside wall at 30m, blooming displays of small sea fans and soft corals are swarming with basslets and chromis, like bees around flowers. Grey reef sharks patrol the whole area – a great thrill if you meet one coming the other way up a channel.

As you ascend for your safety stop, you will move into the richer coral and fish life of the shallows, on the outer edge of the wall. A lucky observer may witness the rare flame angel – once seen, you'll never forget it.

With cruising green and hawksbill turtles, sharks and other life, The Zoo is appropriately named. Each dive yields new species, all within a confined area.

38 MACKAY REEF

Location: *Northwest corner*
Depth Range: *1-5m (3-16ft)*
Access: *Boat to island, entry from beach*
Expertise Rating: *Novice*

Primarily used as a snorkel site, this spot is excellent for keen macrophotographers and snorkelers. The boat drops you on the sandy beach of this cay – submerged on big tides – from which you can adventure out into the shallows between the coral heads and clams, or continue over the edge with scuba.

The bommies come in all sizes, each rich with a different suite of animals and plants. Large colonies of soft corals are seen nearer the island – look at their bases carefully and you will see that some of them are hard. These are made up of the calcium carbonate spines secreted by the soft corals, which are major contributors to back reef growth in the northern GBR.

Giant clams provide a superb range of colours and sizes, with their inhalant and exhalant siphons allowing you to look inside to see their inner workings. Due to small, light-sensitive cells in their mantles, they may sense your shadow as you swim over them, causing them to jerk closed. Other animals here that react by closing up are the many little Christmas tree worms, especially in the boulder coral colonies – their colours are superb.

Turtles are more common than at sites farther offshore, as grazing conditions are generally better. In summer, you may see mating pairs or females waiting around to nest on nearby cays. Anemones and their commensal shrimps and fish are common as well, it is worth examining each anemone carefully for clownfish eggs under its edges. Butterflyfish and surgeons are common and sometimes a large Maori wrasse will cruise in to check you out.

The sand slopes down quickly over the edge, where coral heads provide a continuing range of good animal and plant life. This is a great spot for patient observers.

Small sand cays can be swept away by storms

By searching around, the photographer can gain a great foreground subject

39 | PIXIE'S PINNACLE

Location: *Northwest corner, small plug reef between Ribbons No 9 & 10*
Depth Range: *1-30m (3-98ft)*
Access: *Boat*
Expertise Rating: *Novice*

Pixie's Pinnacle has the best of everything the GBR has to offer. This site can be done in five minutes or, by slowing down, you can see examples of almost every group of organisms found on the GBR.

This coral pinnacle rises from 40m to the surface, where it is about 15m across. By following a slowly descending spiral you will see plenty, finishing with an ascending spiral and a safety stop.

Hard coral diversity is high, with many small colonies striving to fight their way out from under the larger, faster-growing, shading species, especially down to about 20m. Here a talus (rubble) slope starts on all sides, with more soft corals and an occasional large, black (actually dark green) tree coral colony. The slope then drops off slowly at varying angles to a 30m bottom. This is often a resting spot for large cod, feeding sea cucumbers, rays and whitetip reef sharks.

Above the talus slope is a series of vertical walls, overhangs and multitudes of small caves. All provide great hangouts for lionfish, moray eels, shrimp, anemones and their clownfish, cleaner wrasse, hanging spiky soft corals, gorgonians, yellow turret corals, lace corals, sponges, hydroids and molluscs.

On some occasions fairy basslets provide an amazing pink cloud while they feed in the current that bathes the pin-

cruising by or hovering. Fusiliers are regulars, with trevally, barracuda, mackerel, sharks, batfish and the occasional ray providing a charismatic megafaunal experience.

40	**RIBBON REEF No 10 – THE COD HOLE**

Location: *North end of Ribbon No 10*
Depth Range: *10-22m (33-72ft)*
Access: *Boat*
Expertise Rating: *Novice/Intermediate*

Internationally recognised underwater photographers, Ron and Valerie Taylor, were the first to publicise this fantastic fish site, and were instrumental in its declaration as a protected Marine Park Area in the 1970s. Large potato cod (numbers now reported from two to 15 – many less than in the '70s) are friendly, especially since they have been regularly fed for 20 years. Over time, the health of these cod has decreased, with cankers and skin disease becoming evident, possibly due to inappropriate feeding and handling by divers. Today only those with a Marine Parks permit can feed them, and then with special food, so the cod appear to be improving.

Let the divemaster handle any feeding and follow instructions carefully. You dive right off the boat into a cloud of waiting cod, large Maori wrasse, red bass, emperor and many other species, unless they have all been fed by the previous boat, in which case you may only get the stragglers.

You drop to the sandy floor areas between the bommies, which provide amphitheatre-like viewing areas among great coral outcrops, to watch the fish feeding. They generally come close and are superb wide-angle subjects, even if they haven't been fed.

nacle. Many animals are well-camouflaged, such as the resident stonefish, so the patient and observant diver will be rewarded. Be prepared to shoot all your film or fill your memory card, with medium to close-up being your best lens choice.

For those who can tear their eyes away from the life on the pinnacle, there is the reward of shoals of fish regularly

Potato cod are the gentle giants at several popular sites

As with all fed animals, things seem fine at first, but as they grow to expect food, they often lose their ability to forage on their own. If you take food away, they can become aggressive. Cod will mouth and sometimes bite, especially if they haven't been fed for a while, but their thousands of small fine teeth cause only minor lacerations a few millimetres deep.

Tidal currents keep this area interesting and on a rising tide you get much better visibility, making the sandy floors among rich coral heads stand out. If the cod don't show, this is still a great dive, demonstrating a typical back reef channel area.

Other marine life includes excellent coral cover, occasional moray eels, anemones, whitetip reef sharks, giant clams, schools of pyramid butterflyfish, Solomon's sweetlip, cleaning stations and feather stars. At the start of the dive, ensure you know what the bottom of your boat looks like and return to it. If you hear boat engines, watch out for propellers above.

41 · LIZARD ISLAND – COBIA HOLE

Location: *Off point, northeast Watson's Bay*
Depth Range: *14-18m (46-59ft)*
Access: *Boat*
Expertise Rating: *Intermediate*

Home to an exclusive resort with an airstrip and a research station, camping is allowed on Lizard Island with a permit from National Parks.

Your descent at the Cobia Hole takes you onto a submerged mooring float that usually has circling pelagic barracuda or trevally. The cobia have not been seen regularly for years, but watch for them off the rocks or on the sandy bottom at 14m, where you come across a pinnacle of rocks covered with every conceivable group of marine organism.

Macrophotographers will delight in this area, where sponges, soft corals, coralliamorpharians, feather stars, sea stars, sea squirts and their commensal shrimps, crabs and gobies will occupy even the least interested diver. This is best described as another veneer community, where reef life covers the island rock and fish life comes in and occupies the site. Sea whips, gorgonian fans and stinging hydroids with hovering slaty bream can often be seen. The numerous nooks and crannies guarantee a constant supply of more interesting sponges, lace corals and sea squirts.

Often large turtles, toadfish and estuary cod will appear as well. If by some remote chance you run out of subjects on the rocky areas, try looking out on the sea grasses and algae on the nearby sand – make sure your buddy comes and the guide knows where you have gone. There are several other good dives around the island, including the inner lagoon. Snorkeling is popular wherever you can get into the water, as giant clams and corals are common.

The Clam Gardens in Mrs Watson's Bay is a great snorkel between dives at Lizard Island

Silvertip sharks are regular visitors at Osprey Reef

| 42 | **OSPREY REEF – NORTH HORN** |

Location: *Mooring at northwest tip of reef*
Depth Range: *2-20m+ (6-66ft+)*
Access: *Boat*
Expertise Rating: *Intermediate*

Osprey has many sites, with the entrances providing several spots for overnight anchorages and moorings. The North Horn site is best known. Sharks have always been here and a resident population of whitetip reef sharks is currently under study, whereby each one is identified and recorded individually, through the assistance of Undersea Explorer. This site has been used as a shark feeding site for more than 15 years, so the silvertip and grey reef sharks, potato cod, morays and many smaller species are familiar with humans as an irregular food source.

Moorings allow the boat to hang in the safest spot so you dive into water that drops to almost 1000m, with 40m visibility common. The reef edge is an easy 20m swim. Divers gather together at 16 to 20m and when all is set, food is brought down and the action begins. The bolder whitetips come in first, followed by potato cod. Gradually grey reef sharks build up the courage to start feeding and they are closely followed by silvertips. A 45kg dogtooth tuna was once eaten in under 90 seconds, so if you want a photograph – you'll have to be quick!

It is important to follow the divemaster's instructions as they know the usual behavior of these species. Schooling scalloped hammerheads and great hammerheads, possibly seen here seasonally when the waters cool, always bring a feeling of quiet awe.

If you have the time, experience and air, there are some large soft coral trees deep down on the western wall. At this site, you will always see great pelagic action including three-spot dart, dogtooth tuna, rainbow runners and mackerel, with stunning planktonic animals floating by. Snorkeling over the whole wall and nearby reeftop, with its gullies, stinging coral and great fish life, is also a buzz.

Diving nearby sites at night will let you see flashlightfish, pelagic octopus, pleurobranchs, crabs, shrimps and sleeping fish.

As part of its many diving/research expeditions, the Undersea Explorer sometimes trap a nautilus, take its details and then release it, allowing you to observe and swim with it.

Far Northern Reefs

0 ⟩⟩⟩⟩⟩⟩⟩⟩ 8 km
0 ⟩⟩⟩⟩⟩⟩⟩⟩ 4 miles
not for navigation

see inset map

144°E
To Pandora (Dive 47)

Raine Island

Raine Island Entrance

Stead Passage

46 ◣

Yule Detached Reef

12°S

Great Detached Reef

Wishbone Reef

Martha Ridgeway Reefs

Nimrod Passage

Wreck Bay

Safe Entrance

◣ 45

Mantis Reef

Black Rock Entrance

CORAL SEA

Lagoon Reef

Quoin Island Entrance

12°30'S   12°30'S

Long Sandy Reef

Providential Channel

Log Reef

Hibernia Entrance

Bligh Reef

44 ◣

Bligh Boat Entrance

Reef	
Depth	
	0-10m
	10-20m
	20m+

13°S

Cat Reef

Ham Reef

Second 3 Mile Opening

13°S

Colclough Reef

New Reef

Tijou Reef

Diamond Reign Reefs

43 ◣ 144°E

144°E

The tentacles of an anemone

120

Far Northern Reef Dive Sites

A series of sand cays, some vegetated, runs along the outer Far Northern Reefs

As this area extends 300km to 1000km (200 to 600 nautical miles) north of Cairns and Port Douglas, there are no set itinerary diving services to these remote reefs. The area includes all the reefs and islands from Lizard Island to the tip of Cape York, with Torres Strait sites further north. Several boats make annual expeditions and others run charter trips. These reefs are accessible via Cairns, Port Douglas and Cooktown, or you can fly into Lizard Island, Iron Range or Thursday Island to join one of the fly-in, sail-out trips to save the travel time from Cairns or Port Douglas – whatever way you can do it, it is worth it!

About 600 reefs, ranging in size from a few metres across to 35km (22 miles) long and 15km (9 miles) wide, provide thousands of kilometres of diveable reef edges, and that's not including the floors and shoals in between the reefs, or lagoons on their surfaces!

More than one hundred cays and many mainland islands also provide stunning terrestrial experiences. Many are closed or permit-only, due to their status as Aboriginal sites or bird and turtle rookeries. Raine Island once had over 16,000 green turtles nesting there at night and is now an important rookery for turtles, frigate birds, Nankeen night herons, gannets and terns. It is closed at all times.

The reefs best for diving are on the outer edges of the continental shelf, from Lizard Island to adjacent to the tip of Cape York. This gives you a continuous line of ribbon, deltaic and dissected linear (east-west across the shelf) reefs. Visibility is usually 20m (66ft) and up to 50m (165ft). As this shelf edge is from 60km to 160km (35 miles to 100 miles) from the coast, the inshore waters can still be a little dirty from coastal run-off, although there are none of the chemicals and silt from coastal human activities offshore. In the Cape York area, outflows from the Fly River in Papua New Guinea wash down in big floods.

As you get closer to the coast there are more islands, less visibility, more dugong, saltwater crocodiles, tiger sharks and generally less desirable diving conditions. Yet these are fantastic underwater places, if you are at all biologically or muck-diving inclined.

Moving farther north, toward the centre of greatest Indo-Pacific species diversity, it is possible to see as yet undescribed species of corals, fish and

Far Northern Reef Dive Sites	GOOD SNORKELING	NOVICE	INTERMEDIATE	ADVANCED
43 TIJOU REEF – MR WALKER'S CAVES	•			•
44 BLIGH BOAT ENTRANCE	•	•		
45 MANTIS REEF	•	•		
46 GREAT DETACHED REEF	•	•		
47 WRECK OF THE PANDORA			•	

One of the caves in the Mr Walker's Caves complex

other life – these reefs are the richest of the GBR. Generally remote but significantly fished for a long time, these reefs have been subjected to harvesting for beche-de-mer, pearl, trochus, and fishing for coral trout and other reef fish, mud crab and barramundi. However they have been only minimally visited by divers. There are now large 'no trawling or fishing' areas that will hopefully help conserve this area.

All the outer reef edges (channel sides, backs and fronts) are the best known recreational diving areas. Rich corals, pelagic action and great visibility make them memorable.

As boats only usually visit in the late spring and summer months during the monsoonal calms, it is calm enough to dive any part of the reefs, including walls and terraces off reef fronts and sides, which are usually smashed by heavy waves. Your boat operator will take you to the easiest and best-suited sites for your ability and the weather.

Drift dives are often the best way to experience these areas.

Wreck Bay, Great Detached Reef, Raine Island and Pandora Entrance are well known for their manta rays, green turtles, whale shark, sperm whales, Bryde's whales and general pelagic action. There are incredible arrays of coral heads, staghorn thickets, large numbers of fish of all sorts, crayfish, sharks, cascading algal beds, sand falls and giant clams. You can experience almost every conceivable reef feature, along with historical shipwrecks.

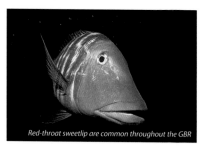

Red-throat sweetlip are common throughout the GBR

43 TIJOU REEF – MR WALKER'S CAVES

Location: *Western wall of southern lagoon*
Depth Range: *1-40m (3-130ft)*
Access: *Boat*
Expertise Rating: *Advanced*

These caves extend along the entire western side of a 55m-deep lagoon on the southern end of Tijou Reef, a ribbon reef 24km-long. Discovered in 1995, they are in a mile-long vertical wall from 20 to 35m. The caves were named in memory of Terry Walker, a great reefie and dive buddy, who lost his life in a boating accident in the Gulf of Carpentaria. The whole reef is a superb site for snorkeling and diving, especially the northern tip at Shark Point.

The only access to the lagoons and caves is over the reeftop. If the boat anchors on the western side, numerous small coral heads and patches on sand provide excellent snorkeling in 1m to 5m, and become an exciting drift in tide runs. If the boat anchors on the outside, there is a shelf of reef that is also excellent for snorkeling and scuba.

The lagoon is unusual because of both its depth and the caves. Entry into most of the caves is okay, but some are quite complex and need ropes, so be very careful or trained and follow procedures. Funds are being raised to undertake research into the cave sediment, to determine if there is a break in layers between the terrestrial sediment of the last ice age and an overlay of marine sediment since resubmergence. To date, researchers have cored to 3m and found sediment more than 3000 years old.

The wall is vertical with numerous gullies and overhangs. A sand-and-rubble slope at its base leads onto the gently sloping sandy lagoon floor. On the eastern side of the lagoon, a larger sand slope extends from 1m to 5m to the floor. Two large bommies rich in coral and fish provide good diving and snorkeling.

In late November sharks in large numbers have been observed, possibly breeding, as their behaviour was highly aggressive. Usually a few grey reef sharks appear on each dive. Trevally, barracuda and numerous reef species are seen along the wall. Triggerfish are common, especially on sandy floor areas.

44 BLIGH BOAT ENTRANCE

Location: *Wall along southern side of channel*
Depth Range: *1-35m (3-115ft)*
Access: *Boat*
Expertise Rating: *Intermediate*

On the northern tip of reef no#12-127 and south of Bligh Reef is the entrance that Captain Bligh and 18 shipmates, sailing in the *Bounty* long boat, used in their 3618 nautical mile epic journey from Tonga to Timor. Little did they know that only 200 years later this would become one of the premier dive sites in the region!

This site is best dived as a drift on the incoming tide. You enter at the notch about a third of the way in and drop to your planned depth. Sometimes eddies can swing you out into the chan-

Bligh's Boat Passage is historic and a great dive site

nel or apparently the wrong way. In this case, go with the flow but be careful as it is very easy to go below depth here. You end the dive at the reef point by popping around the corner and doing a safety stop in the shallows, where the coral is excellent.

Along the wall, photographers can shoot wide-angle and enjoy the enormous plate and staghorn corals, gorgonian fans, silvertip and grey reef sharks and barracuda that occasionally cruise here. Alternately, go macro for the great diversity of small life to be seen. Feather stars hang out in the current for food, while huge swirling schools of basslets, parrotfish, wrasse, surgeonfish and damsels provide a disorienting effect – especially towards the end of the dive. Large soft corals, whips and black tree coral colonies are common.

As the wall is so sharp it has small gutters nearer the surface, sand falls and algal cascades occur in-between the corals and small gully floors. Look for resting whitetip or tawny sharks.

 45   MANTIS REEF

Location: *Northwest end of Mantis Reef*
Depth Range: *1-40m+ (3-130ft+)*
Access: *Boat*
Expertise Rating: *Intermediate*

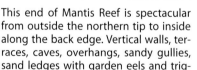

This end of Mantis Reef is spectacular from outside the northern tip to inside along the back edge. Vertical walls, terraces, caves, overhangs, sandy gullies, sand ledges with garden eels and triggerfish nests and shallow bommies add up to excellent diving at many sites.

Outside, on the front, a vertical face stretches almost all along the 19km of the reef. This is where more of the great pelagic action is seen, with barracuda schools, trevally and fusiliers. Sperm whales and whale sharks have also been spotted. Potato cod and gropers are resident and, deeper down, enormous gorgonian fans and spiky soft corals reach out into the waters. Keep an eye out for manta and mobula rays.

If you are snorkeling, the sandy flat area around shallow bommies at the reef back is superb as a coral garden site. Butterflyfish, damsels, angelfish, triggerfish and flutemouths will be often seen. Cod, trout and surgeonfish are common, especially in among the staghorn and plate corals.

It is important here that you plan your dive and your plan well, due to the remoteness of the site, depths and currents. It is worth it!

46   GREAT DETACHED REEF

Location: *Northwest GDR reef, western edge*
Depth Range: *2-40m+ (7-130ft)*
Access: *Boat*
Expertise Rating: *Intermediate or Advanced*

Great Detached Reef is a large complex of several reefs on an older fossil surface. There are numerous reported shipwrecks on the reeftop – many known and many still unknown. This reef has about 46km (27 miles) of edge – dive sites are innumerable. The northwest site is representative of all sites and convenient for anchorage.

Far Northern Reefs generally give great visibility

Pink sponges compete with soft coral for food from the currents

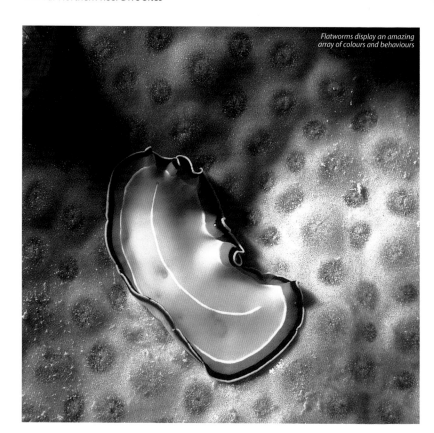

Flatworms display an amazing array of colours and behaviours

Diving from the boat, you can go to either side of a small coral promontory that extends westward from the reef. The surface of this reef is at 2m and two swim-throughs allow you to cross from side-to-side. One is closed over the top but easily traversed. Closer to the back edge of the main reef are giant clams and coral gardens of staghorn and plate corals, in about 8m.

On either side of the ridge an almost vertical wall drops away 200m. Superb pelagics, including barracuda, trevally and sharks, cruise by constantly. Schools of basslets, fusiliers and sometimes blue-lined snapper are also to be found.

Soft spiky coral and gorgonians add to the colour, as do feather stars. Stinging coral is common, so be careful. Watch your depths and stick close to the walls for orientation.

47	PANDORA WRECK

Location: *Sea floor to north of Pandora Entrance*
Depth Range: *33-36m (100-110ft)*
Access: *Boat*
Expertise Rating: *Intermediate or Advanced*

Internationally significant, the HMS *Pandora* is the oldest known wreck off Australia's east coast. She is best known as the Royal Navy frigate sent by the British Admiralty to pursue *Bounty* mutineers. After nearly five months searching the South Pacific, the *Pandora* was on her way home from Tahiti with 14 prisoners – mutineers along with several *Bounty* crew who couldn't fit on Bligh's longboat.

They were locked in a makeshift cell, 'Pandora's Box', on the ship's quarterdeck. While exploring a passage through the GBR, the *Pandora* struck a reef on 28 August 1791. She sank the next morning in 33m (108ft). Of the 35 people who died, four were *Bounty* mutineers.

The ship remains have been extensively investigated on expeditions by Queensland Museum staff, other professionals and volunteers. The results of the project are on display in a spectacular Maritime Archaeology gallery at the Museum of Tropical Queensland in Townsville.

The copper sheathing off the stern post of the Pandora sits proud of the bottom

Pandora Wreck

The Queensland Museum chose to dedicate so much effort to the *Pandora* due to its historical importance and archaeological potential. About a quarter of the wreck is exceptionally well preserved, although it is buried under sand, so very little can be seen. The fascinating array of recovered artefacts enables the museum to reconstruct a rare view of what life was like onboard an 18th-century European ship. This ambitious effort – the *Pandora* Project – was funded by government departments and the *Pandora* Foundation, established to ensure the success of this exciting maritime archaeological project.

To dive the site you must go with a permitted operator who meets strict requirements. Permit applications can be directed to the Museum of Tropical Queensland in Townsville (☎ 07 4726 0625). Alternately, an application form can be downloaded from www.mtq.qld.gov.au.

Once at the wreck site, you drop straight down to 33m (108ft). Visibility allowing, you can see the stern anchor and sheathing, the bow anchor and the nearby oven, which are the most obvious features. In-between is a hard-to-discern coral-covered cannon, swivel guns, a chain pump and many unidentified concretions. A consecrated obelisk on the southeast corner is where one of the skeletons excavated so far was found.

The dive enlists your sense of history and imagination of the *Pandora's* voyage more than 200 years ago. The top three-quarters of the wooden hull have been eaten away by Teredo worms, leaving the ship filled with Halimeda algae sands, which buried artefacts that slid down into the hull. Poles and frames allow archaeologists to accurately determine where each excavated artefact came from. Shoals of fish mix with the algae and coral that shroud most of the wreck's remains.

Tube worms have an enormous range of breathing and feeding appendages

Torres Strait

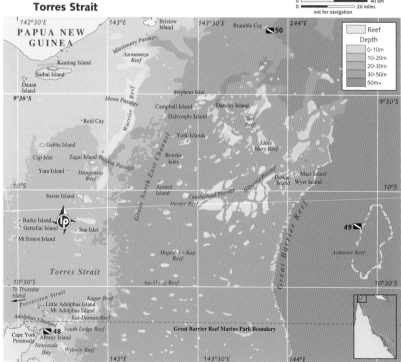

0 — 40 km
0 — 20 miles
not for navigation

Reef

Depth
0-10m
10-20m
20-30m
30-50m
50m+

PAPUA NEW GUINEA

142°30'E *143°E* Bristow Island *143°30'E* Bramble Cay **50** *144°E*

Missionary Passage

Auwamaza Reef

Kaumag Island

Saibai Island

Dauan Island

Stephens Islet

9°30'S Moon Passage Campbell Island Darnley Island *9°30'S*

Reid Cay Dalrymple Island Sen Reef

Warrior Reef York Islands Little Mary Reef

Gabba Island

Cap Islet Zagai Island Basilisk Passage Bourke Isles

Yam Island Dungeness Reef

Great North East Channel Dowar Island Maer Island Wyer Island

Sassie Island Aureed Island Cumberland Passage

Derder Reef

Burke Island **48** Sue Islet

Gettullai Island

Mt Ernest Island

49

Maped-Au-Kap Reef Ashmore Reef

Torres Strait

Great Barrier Reef

10°30'S Au-Masig Reef *10°30'S*

To Thursday Island

Possession Strait Kagar Reef

Little Adolphus Island

Mt Adolphus Island

Adolphus Channel Kai-Damun Reef

Cape York Peninsula South Ledge Reef **Great Barrier Reef Marine Park Boundary**

Albany Island

Newcastle Bay Wyborn Reef

143°E *143°30'E* *144°E*

Torres Strait Dive Sites

Torres Strait includes significant parts of the GBR, mainland islands, reefs and cays. The strait connects the Coral and Arafura Seas, which are part of the Pacific and Indian Oceans. Anchor Cay, **Bramble Cay** and Black Rocks make up the northernmost point of the GBR.

The Torres Strait has a reasonably high tide range (4m) and receives the massive freshwater outflow of Papua New Guinea's Fly River. There are strong currents and sediment-rich waters, and the tides are complex and can be hazardous to shipping. Access is via the airport on Horn Island, which is adjacent to Thursday Island, the primary port and administration centre for the area.

Leading into the most diverse reef system in the world (the Sunda Sea in Indonesia), Torres Strait is the richest part of the GBR Province and is also the most diverse area in its island and reef morphology. To the east are the Ashmore and Boot Reef complexes, also part of the Coral Sea Reefs.

This region features large platform reefs (up to 28km (17 miles) long) over mud and sand bases, with islands of mud, sand and shingle. There are mainland islands with fringing reefs and many reefs with sand cays. Many islands are inhabited by Torres Strait Islanders, who are of Melanesian descent. Rich sea grass communities, mangroves, soft bottoms and reefs provide for the varied fish, dugong and turtle populations.

A long history of pearl, trochus and beche-de-mer industries provide insight into the area's colourful past, as evident in the cemetery on Thursday Island. Recreational diving opportunities are limited and only offered by a few boats due to the general misconception that diving is undesirable in this area. The western straits are in shal-

Butterfly fish with their bright colours distract all divers

lower muddy waters and are unlikely to ever become popular as dive destinations. The eastern straits provide excellent and unique diving opportunities, which will probably gain popularity as services develop.

Rare pulses of deep oceanic water slide in under Torres Strait waters decreasing visibility and temperature. Common features include walls, slopes, lagoons, caves and channels. Further west, a scattering of reefs have incredible potential as dive sites. Large sharks, whale sharks, turtles and pelagic fish are often seen.

Torres Strait Dive Sites	GOOD SNORKELING	NOVICE	INTERMEDIATE	ADVANCED
48 RMS QUETTA				•
49 ASHMORE REEF – WESTERN EDGE	•	•		
50 BRAMBLE CAY	•	•		

Christmas tree worms dart back into their tubes at the slightest disturbance

48   RMS QUETTA

Location: *East of Cape York, eastern side of Adolphus Channel*
Depth Range: *10-24m (33-79ft)*
Access: *Boat*
Expertise Rating: *Advanced*

Divers require a permit to dive this historic site. Strong tidal currents and generally low visibility present a difficult dive, making it necessary to have accurate tide information to plan the 20 minutes of slack water at high or low tide. It is common for divers to be swept away either entry or exit, so have your pick-up boats, safety sausages and systems well planned.

The wreck, or at least its ripple effect in the current, can sometimes be seen from the surface. Descent brings you into contact with a ship that is still in reasonably good condition and covered with prolific marine life. Thousands of fish move over, in and around the wreck.

It would be possible to penetrate parts of the wreck, but is dangerous to do so and certainly no longer safe.

Like the *Yongala* and the *Gothenberg*, the RMS *Quetta* (1890) was a passenger ship that lost more than 100 lives. Unlike the others, however, the *Quetta* was not lost during a cyclone but rather sank after striking an uncharted rock off Mount Adolphus Island. It took just three minutes, taking 133 of her 290 passengers and crew with her.

Seasoned wreck divers argue that the *Quetta* is actually a more spectacular wreck dive than the *Yongala*. Access to the *Quetta* is difficult – and expensive, not only because of its remote location, but mainly because it is exposed to strong currents. All divers should be wary here and it is highly recommended that you dive at slack water.

As is the case with diving on the *Pandora*, unless you have a private vessel, access is easiest by charter dive boat from either Cairns or Port Douglas, where a variety of dive charter operators offer extended 'dive safari' tours to the far northern GBR.

The stern lies well-exposed showing the propeller and rudder. Until you reach the enormous gash low on the bow, she seems almost intact.

Remnants of funnels, masts and other equipment lie scattered around the site. This is a significant wreck with many items, including the bell, on display at the Quetta Cathedral on Thursday Island.

Sadly, many artefacts had been removed from this important site prior to its protection as a historic site. Any seen during your dive should be left alone, photographed and reported to the Museum of Tropical Queensland.

49 ASHMORE REEF – WESTERN EDGE

Location: *Western edge of complex*
Depth Range: *1-30m (3-98ft)*
Access: *Boat*
Expertise Rating: *Novice/Intermediate*

This outer slope is connected to the lagoon interior through channels. Rich staghorn corals group with the big branching blue and brown colonies and many table growth forms. This richness extends to 30m with the species changing away from the staghorn group to big fleshy polyp forms and hat corals up to 1m across. The walls have rubble slopes at the bases and rich growths of hard and soft corals, with whips, gorgonians and stinging coral.

Large silvertip, grey reef and whitetip reef sharks, along with other species of whaler sharks, are common and inquisitive but leave quickly if you rush them. Large pelagic species of mackerel, blue trevally, barracuda and tuna are regulars, along with fusiliers, damsels, wrasse and parrotfish. Basslets and other open ocean reef species are common with garden eels poking their heads out of the 15-30m sand ledges.

Outer and Coral Sea Reefs are enormously varied in their diversity of coral covers

This is a good site for wide-angle photography but sometimes pulses of dirty water will push you to macro systems. Several species of sea snakes are also seen here and as always are inquisitive but safer if left alone. There are ample shallow coral areas for safety stops and snorkeling.

50 BRAMBLE CAY

Location: *Northeast edge of reef*
Depth Range: *1-25m (3-82ft)*
Access: *Boat*
Expertise Rating: *Novice*

Bramble Cay is the northernmost reef of the GBR. It has a sand cay, with low plant growth and a light tower, and is an important turtle nesting rookery for green turtles.

Many dive site possibilities exist around the reef. The southeastern side drops down to sand flats at 12m to 30m with some walls, lots of rubble slopes and sediment-resistant coral species. The diversity of coral is high but the coverage is often low. Large beds of daytime coral cover areas up to 80m long and 5m wide. Low visibility can make it a macro-photography site.

Balls of boulder corals are alive on every surface, indicating they are rolled around by the strong wave and/or current action. The rubble slopes have many encrusting colonies of lettuce corals with free-living species of mushrooms and their cousins.

On the wall sections, which drop from 3m to 10m, there are many boulder, elephant skin and soft corals. Whip and gorgonian corals are common as well. As this area is rich in algae, there are also many grazing fish, especially rabbitfish and wrasse with trumpetfish, unicornfish and surgeons equally abundant.

Yellow turret coral is common under overhangs and in wrecks

A tubed anemone provides the photographer with a soft contrast to the hard coral overhang above

Marine Life

Schools of barracuda are common and can be seen at many sites

The GBR (and additionally the tropical coral reefs to the near north) is one of the few places you can see representatives from almost every group of animal on the planet – and many you won't see anywhere else. The greatest challenge is to identify and name these millions of animals so other divers know what you are talking about.

The system biologists use to differentiate one critter from another is known as binomial nomenclature – the method of using two words (usually shown in italics) to identify an organism. The second word is the species, which is the finest detail name for an animal, and refers to organisms that can only breed with other members of the same species. The first italic word is the genus, into which members of similar species are grouped. Where the species or genus is unknown, the naming goes to the next known (and less specific) level: Family (F), Order (O), Class (C) and Phylum (P).

For real animal knowledge it is best to choose one animal and observe it closely. It is too easy to try to look at everything at once. A slate is a very good way of remembering shapes or colour patterns.

The vertebrates (animals with backbones) in the photographs below show some of the most common members of the major families. Use these shapes as the basis of your slate diagrams.

Invertebrates are animals that have no backbone at any time of their life. Invertebrates are by far the most diverse animals seen anywhere, especially underwater. The photographs below show the major groups and their evolutionary sequence of development and complexity.

whale shark
Rhincodon typus

leopard shark
Stegostoma fasciatum

whitetip reef shark
Triaenodon obesus

grey reef shark
Carcharhinus amblyrhyncos

Photo: John Barnett

scalloped hammerhead shark
Sphyrna lewini

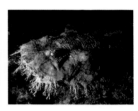

tassled wobbegong
Eucrossorhinus dasypogon

cowtail ray
Pastinachus sephen

manta ray
Manta birostris

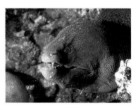

giant moray eel
Gymnothorax javanicus

variegated lizardfish
Synodus variegatus

reef flounder
F. Cynoglossidae

painted flutemouth
Aulostomus chinensis

spotfin lionfish
Pterois antennata

potato cod
Epinephelus tukula

coral trout
Plectropomus leopardus

redthroat sweetlip
Lethrinus miniatus

yellowfin goatfish
Mulloidichthys vanicolensis

longfin bannerfish
Heniochus acuminatus

beaked coralfish
Chelmon rostratus

blue angelfish
Pomacanthus semicirculatus

flame angelfish
Centropyge loriculus

pink anemonefish
Amphiprion perideraion

green moon wrasse
Thalassoma lutescens

Maori wrasse
Cheilinus undulatus

minifin parrotfish
Scarus altipinnis

clown triggerfish
Balistoides conspicillum

black-spotted toadfish
Arothon nigropunctatus

Clouds of planktiverous fish show the presence
of rich microscopic food in the passing waters

sponge
Amphimedron sp.

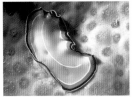

flatworm
Pseudoceros bimarginatus

feather duster worm
Protula sp.

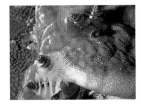

Christmas tree worm
Spirobranchus giganteus

turret corals
Tubastraea sp.

comb gorgonian
Ctenocella pectinata

zoanthid
Palythoa sp.

tubed anemone
F. Ceriantidae

black coral
Atipathes sp.

staghorn coral
Acropora sp.

soft coral
Dendronephthya sp.

lace coral
Stylaster sp.

painted crayfish
Panulirus versicolor

imperial shrimp
Periclemes imperator

egg cowry
Ovula ovum

octopus
Octopus sp.

giant clam
Tridacna gigas

chromodoris nudi-branch
Chromodoris coi

rigid-bodied nudibranch
Notodoris gardineri

bryozoans
Phyl. Bryozoa

feather star
Cl. Crinoidea

blue sea star
Linckia laevigata

sea cucumber
Thelanota anax

sea urchin
Echinometra mathaei

Divers can explore every possible reef habitat on the GBR

Box sea jellies are only found in costal waters during northerly calms

HAZARDOUS MARINE LIFE

Marine animals almost never attack divers, but many have defensive and offensive weaponry that can be triggered if they feel threatened or annoyed. If you're not sure what something is, don't touch it! Being able to recognise potentially hazardous creatures is a good way to avoid accident or injury. The following photographs illustrate some of the GBR's most venomous and dangerous marine life, followed by short descriptions of what to expect and some recommendations for first aid in the unfortunate event you are stung, bitten or stabbed. Trained locals are aware of the latest discoveries in terms of the animals and what treatments are best.

Bristle worms

Bristle worms are free-living polychaete (many-bristled) worms. If you touch one, its bristles will break off in your skin, causing an intense burning sensation. Using gently applied glue or wax will help remove the fine, hair-like bristles.

Sea jellies & other stingers

Sea jellies, box jellies and Portuguese man-o-war are found in GBR waters and have dangerous tentacles loaded with nematocysts (stinging cells), used to deter predators and catch prey. Upon contact, the stinging cells will 'fire' and cut into the skin, injecting venom.

Box jellies are found only along the coast. They, and the small Irukandji (a type of box jelly), can deliver fatal stings. However, deaths are uncommon and even severe stings can usually be treated with modern first aid. Flood sea jelly stings with vinegar and the recommended fluid for that species, then apply a cold compress. For others, remove any remaining tentacles with forceps, flood the wound with iced water and maintain a cold compress.

Fire coral

Fire coral appears as two basic hydrozoan forms. Fireweed can be either white or brown and is soft, fragile and feathery. The hard form – stinging coral – is either encrusting or branching and appears as a yellow or brown colony. Look at them carefully and you will see their surfaces are covered in tiny hairs – each loaded with stinging cells. The hairs grow out of minute pores, hence its scientific name, Millepora. Contact results in a burning itch which may develop into secondary infections if scratched. To treat, use vinegar then hydrocortisone cream.

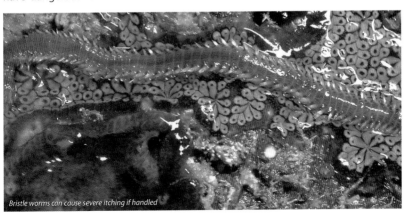
Bristle worms can cause severe itching if handled

Corallimorpharian

Anemones & Corallimorpharians

Anemones and corallimorpharians use the same stinging cells as the fire corals and sea jellies. Some anemones are totally harmless, while others can cause a severe pain or allergic reaction. Corallimorpharian stings tend to be itchier and take much longer to heal. Treat with vinegar, ice packs and local anesthetics and monitor the patient.

Cone shells

Cone shells are found in the shallows of most reeftops and under boulders. These attractive shells are armed with a proboscis, out of which shoots a small poisonous harpoon used to inject a highly toxic venom. In the event of a sting, the stung area will go numb, and can be followed by muscular or respiratory paralysis and even, in extreme cases, heart failure. Treat as for snake bite with a pressure bandage and seek medical attention immediately.

Blue-ringed octopus

Although only small – 5cm to 20cm – this octopus, whose blue rings flash when it is annoyed, delivers a sometimes fatal bite which can cause death if EAR is not maintained. People have put shells in their wetsuit only to be surprised when a blue-ringed octopus emerges. Avoid empty shells, cans, bottles and the octopus. Apply pressure bandages and seek medical attention.

Sea urchins & Crown-of-thorns sea stars

With spines strong enough to penetrate neoprene and the skin, spiny sea urchins and crown-of-thorns sea stars are obvious creatures to avoid, especially urchin species that have a toxin bulb at the end of the spines. Some urchins have toxic pedicellariae (pincers) between the spines, which cause severe pain upon contact and have killed humans. Like most hazardous critters, you can completely avoid injury by not touching them. To treat, remove the spine debris and soak affected area in non-scalding hot water.

Sea snakes

The venom of these air-breathing reptiles is said to be up to 20 times stronger than any land snake. Sea snakes only release venom when feeding or under extreme distress – so most defensive bites do not contain venom. If bitten and injected with venom, immobilise the limb, use a pressure bandage and get help immediately. Do not wash the wound.

Stingrays

Stingrays are generally harmless but be careful when walking in the shallows or kneeling on the bottom. If you tread on a ray, it will flick its tail over its head and drive the barb in its tail downward into your leg or foot. The barb can penetrate bone and leaves venom, which is extremely painful. Remove any debris and put the wounded area into non-scalding hot water. This denatures the venom in about 20 minutes. Always shuffle your feet when walking in the shallows and check the sea floor before kneeling.

Sharks

Sharks have never killed nor injured a scuba diver in GBR waters. There have been a few bumps and rubs – causing skin abrasions or lacerations – but most sharks are totally harmless. The few that have the size to be potentially harmful are usually timid. Incidents usually only occur to people intentionally feeding sharks or carrying fish, which sharks can try to take for food. Townsville has one of the highest death rates to sharks in the world – but all occurred during WWII when soldiers swam in the river outlet that carried offal from the local meat works!

Moray eels

Morays open and close their mouths to breathe, which makes them look as though they're about to take a big bite. But, shy by nature, morays will leave you alone if you leave them alone. They will bite in unusual circumstances and when they do it is difficult to get them to let go, as their teeth slant backwards. If bitten treat the wound with antiseptics then seek medical attention.

Barracuda

All teeth and almost no bite, barracuda often get a bad rap. Unless provoked, they rarely attack divers. They may be attracted to a shiny object resembling a lure. They have sharp, backward-slanting teeth and an underslung jaw, which allows them to hang on. If you are bitten, don't pull back too quickly thus avoiding nasty tears to the skin. Treat as you would a moray bite.

Venomous fish

Scorpionfish, stonefish and lionfish are all masters-of-disguise with bulbs of venom at the base of their dorsal spines (or all spines in the case of the lionfish), so if you tread on one or annoy it enough, you are likely to be punctured and then injected with venom. Use non-scalding hot water to denature the venom and seek medical advice.

Dusk dives allow you to see the 'change of shifts' as the daytime species go to sleep and the night feeders come out

Travel Facts

Modern wave-piercing catamarans speed day visitors to many reefs
Photo: www.quicksilvergroup.com.au

GETTING THERE

Australia is well serviced with international flights. Brisbane and Cairns are the international ports with regular domestic services to all the GBR points. The state of Queensland has many coastal centres with regular commuter air services that serve as jumping-off points to the GBR and Coral Sea. Australia's major domestic airlines will book and supply services to all ports (including services run by subsidiary airlines).

Lady Elliot, Brampton, Hamilton, Dunk, Lizard and Hicks Islands all have their own airstrips, as do many of the Torres Strait Islands. There are feeder airports at Bundaberg, Gladstone, Mackay, Proserpine, Townsville, Cairns and Thursday (Horn) Island. Iron Range has an airstrip, which is often used as a change-over point for Far Northern GBR expedition trips through Portland Roads, serviced from either Cairns or Thursday Island.

Cairns – The GBR's Gateway City

With a population of more than 100,000, Cairns is now firmly established as one of Australia's top travel destinations and is the main jumping-off port to GBR and Coral Sea destinations.

Cairns was once a laid-back country town, but today is a modern, vivacious city that lives and breathes tourism. Cairns Airport is one of the busiest in Australia and the flow of international arrivals continues to swell.

Many divers start or finish their GBR trip in Cairns and, although the city itself only has a small built beach, dozens of operators run daily and hourly trips to nearby beaches and offshore islands and reefs. Cairns is also the centre for a host of other activities including whitewater rafting, para-sailing, rainforest excursions, horse-riding, hiking, mountain biking, canoeing and, for the real adrenaline junkies, there's always bungee jumping or sky diving.

Dive training occurs in many GBR locations

GETTING AROUND

In most major centres there are regular bus services (check with the local tourist or information centre for fares and schedules) and taxis are everywhere, but can get expensive if you have a lot of running around to do before your dive trip. Renting a car is a good option if you have a group of people, enjoy driving long distances and have the time. Plan carefully as the distances between cities are deceptively long. Rental cars are available at every centre and airport, while some long-stay visitors even buy a car for the duration of their visit.

Coaches (most with movies), operate regularly between all centres and are the backpacker's choice of transport. The coaches are met by backpacker representatives at most towns. You can take a train from Brisbane to Cairns – an inexpensive and a great way to see the countryside if you have the time. Cruises between Townsville and Cairns, or Cairns and Cooktown are a great travel option, although diving is often a lower priority to cruising, snorkeling and island visits.

Many dive operators offer a pickup service from local accommodations. Helicopters, floatplanes and amphibians can also take you directly to islands, boats or reef pontoons. Most are on a charter basis but some have regular services. A great site, listing current opportunities and services, is www.queenslandholidays.com.au.

Dive briefs can be the most important part of your dive

MONEY

Australia uses Australian dollars and cents only. Generally all other currencies are only acceptable at banks. Traveller's cheques can be used but usually at a poorer rate at retail outlets. The use of credit cards is easy and widespread and there are many -hole in the wall' ATMs and Eftpos outlets, which will work with most overseas accounts. All dive services and accommodations accept credit cards.

TIME

Australian Eastern Standard Time (GBR) is 10 hours ahead of GMT except on Heron Island Resort, which is 11 hours ahead. Queensland does not observe daylight saving time seen in other Australian states. When it's noon on the GBR, it's 11am in Tokyo, 2am in London and 6pm the day before in San Francisco. World times are listed under 'International Codes' in the local telephone directories.

ELECTRICITY

Three-pin flat-point plugs are standard in Australia. All electricity is on a 240V, 50Hz cycle, available at all resorts and on overnight vessels. As most are on a generator system, fluctuations are common so be careful with sensitive gear. Check ahead if you require 110V as it is rarely available. If you need multiple outlets, bring along a multi-plug 'power board,' converter plugs and a transformer. Most duty free, hardware and luggage stores have converter plugs. Under no circumstances should you plug a non-240V unit into any Australian outlet.

WEIGHTS & MEASURES

Australia follows the metric system, although many people still understand imperial systems. In this book, both

ENTRY

To visit Australia you need a current passport valid for three months after your departure. For visa requirements, visit www.immi.gov.au or check with your local Australian consulate.

DIVING LAWS

International standards apply. To dive in Queensland you need to show your dive certification card and log book. Operators will often want to chat about what diving you have done. You will often be asked to sign a waiver form to protect the operator.

If you wish to undertake a resort or introductory dive you are required to complete a medical questionnaire – ideally you should have a proper medical by a diving doctor as there are particular aspects to diving physiology that diving doctors are trained in.

Current laws governing diving in Queensland are listed on www.dir.qld.gov.au/workplace/subjects/diving.

Anemonefish are very brave amongst the stinging tentacles of their host anemone
Photo: Michael Aw

imperial and metric measurements are given, except for specific references to depth, which are given in metres. Be careful to plan and undertake your dives in whatever system your gauges use. Divemasters are almost always capable of handling both measurements, but it's good to know what you're using before you head out. Refer to the conversion chart at the back of this book.

WHAT TO BRING

Bring prescription medicines. It's also wise to carry copies of the prescriptions in case you need more, or to subdue an over-enthusiastic customs person. Carry them with you and even carry another set in your luggage in case of loss. Some drugs sold overseas are not available in Australia or are known under different names, so it's important to know what the drug is. Also bring prescription lenses, and their prescriptions and any other hard-to-get items. Other personal items are readily available in major centres along the coast.

It can get cold and windy at sea and on the islands, so a good waterproof windbreaker or spray jacket is useful. A woolen sweater or fleece is advisable during winter in the south. A hat, sunglasses, sunscreen, long-sleeved shirt or rashie for sunburn protection is also important – there are reasons for the famous Aussie hats! Bug repellent is useful on the coast and some islands.

DIVE-RELATED EQUIPMENT

For long periods of diving, you'll find a light wetsuit (3mm) is suitable throughout the north. In the south, in winter to early summer, you'll want a 5mm full wetsuit, hood and boots. A lycra skin is ideal for snorkeling and sun protection. Most operators rent out equipment at prices similar to most international destinations. Wetsuits are usually in good order. With competition and the high standards required by Queensland law, most operators now carry only well-serviced gear and offer computers in the rental package. As each operator is

In addition to the cheery 'g'day' and friendly 'how ya goin' mate?' you'll hear a variety of distinctly Aussie words, even in the universal language of diving. Here are just a few:

Barra – barramundi
Body condom / party frock – wetsuit
Bommie – an isolated coral head
Bugs – shovel-nosed lobster
Cod – grouper
Cobia – kingfish
Darwin stubby – one gallon bottle of beer
FILO divers – first-in-last-out
Groper – grouper or over-enthusiastic diver of the opposite sex
Hot boat – when a dive boat drops divers off without anchoring or mooring
Laughing gear – mouth
LIFO divers – last-in-first-out
Little men in grey suits – sharks
Rubber duck – inflatable boat
Parachute entry – this is when divers line up and follow each other into the water, like parachutists out of an aircraft. This is done from a hot boat.
Port – suitcase (short for 'portmanteau')
Shark biscuits – novice surfers
Trevally – jacks
Stubby – small bottle of beer
Tinnie – can of beer or aluminum boat
Togs – swimsuit
Torch – flashlight
Wobby – wobbegong shark

Careful divers monitor their air usage

and a dive computer. Divers should also use the DCIEM (Defence & Civil Institute of Environmental Medicine) tables and follow the instructions of the Divemaster. Be patient with dive staff, as the precautions are for your safety and protection.

Repairs are readily available at coastal centres but generally not on boats or at resorts. Most locations sell all dive equipment, books and videos. Purchasing spare parts here can be risky, as most retail centres cater to a limited range of brands. Batteries are available almost everywhere.

BUSINESS HOURS

different, check beforehand (in writing if possible), to ensure you are getting the gear or air mixes you want.

The basic principles of safe diving are enshrined in law. Queensland law says that each diver must dive with a buddy, wear a BC with a whistle, have an alternate air source, gauges, a protection suit, weights with a quick release catch

Almost everything is open from 9am to 5pm Monday to Friday, except for banks, which are open to 4pm, and 5pm only on Fridays. Most shops open 9am to noon on Saturdays, with major shopping centres open all day Saturday and some on Sunday. For specialty items, it's best to shop before the weekend, when many specialty shops are closed.

ACCOMMODATION

Stay in a deluxe all-inclusive resort or pitch your tent on a remote reef island – accommodations on the GBR run the full gamut. Four to five star accommodations are available in Port Douglas, Cairns, Townsville and on Heron, Hayman, Dunk, Bedarra and Lizard islands. There are also four-star hotels in Mission Beach, Airlie Beach, Mackay, Yeppoon, Rockhampton, Gladstone and Bundaberg. Motels, hotels, caravan parks, camping areas and backpackers (privately run budget hostels) are available at all centres and many places in between. Most dive operators will be happy to suggest affiliated accommodations or suggest a hotel that has the best deal for your requirements. Keep in mind that June and July are peak tourism months, with school holidays falling at this time, and prices can vary depending on when you go.

Many of the islands are national parks and with a permit from the Environment Protection Agency you can camp at minimal cost. Some islands – such as Great Keppel, Magnetic, Hook and Fitzroy islands – have hostels or other forms of budget accommodations. For details and permits, visit www.epa.qld.gov.au/parks_and_forests. Many operators can organise accommodation for divers as part of a package.

DINING & FOOD

Port Douglas has the reputation for the best dining available on the GBR coast, but there's still a good range of restaurants around Cairns, Townsville and the Whitsundays. Popular seafood dishes include barramundi (found in rivers and estuaries in northern Australia), coral trout, tuna, sweetlip, bream and mangrove jack. Fresh prawns, Moreton Bay bugs, painted crayfish and mud-crab are also popular. Excellent Australian wines are available, as are local beers like VB and XXXX (four-ex, because it is said they couldn't spell beer!) – a favourite after a hot day on the reef. For dessert try the pavlova – an 'Australian' dessert made of meringue, whipped cream and fruit – it was invented in New Zealand, they say!

THINGS TO BUY

Australia is a signatory to the CITES (Convention on International Trade in Endangered Species) Convention so it is illegal to trade in turtle shell, dugong, many shells, coral, black coral and the like. Treat your time on the reef as a national park experience and limit yourself to souvenirs such as T-shirts, videos, books, your own photos and your dive log. Items made from marine organisms (jewellery, shell etc) that are for sale in shops were probably obtained legally. It's likely that these items were collected in a non-sustainable fashion and to the detriment of their environment – your future dive sites. Sunscreens, clothes, confectionery, film, books, batteries and the like are available at most resort boutiques and on many boats.

Townsville is one of several cosmopolitan centres allowing easy access to the GBR

Anemonefish are always a delight to see as they dash in and out of their host anemone's tentacles

Listings

Small red sea stars are great macro subjects and commonly seen out grazing on the substrate.

To call Australia, dial the international access code for the country you are calling from. From the US it's 011 + 61 (Australia's country code) + 7 (Queensland's area code) + the eight-digit local number.

DIVE SERVICES

We suggest you only use members of Queensland Dive Tourism Association, which shows a commitment to professional activities, safety and services. Visit www.dive-queensland.com.au for operator listings.

Also check that your chosen operator is a member of the Ecotourism Association of Australia (www.ecotourism.org.au/index.asp). The Eco Certification Program was developed to address the need to identify genuine ecotourism and nature tourism operators in Australia.

BUNDABERG

Bundaberg Aqua Scuba
Shop 1/66 Targo St
Bundaberg, QLD 4670
☎ 07 4153 5761
www.aquascuba.com.au

GLADSTONE

Voyagers Mountain & Marine
PO Box 616
Gladstone, QLD 4680
☎ 07 4972 9055
www.voyages.com.au

AIRLIE BEACH

Mantaray Charters
PO Box 140
Airlie Beach, QLD 4802
☎ 07 4948 1511
www.mantaraycharters.com

Oceania Dive
PO Box 1060
Airlie Beach, QLD 4802
☎ 07 4946 7446
www.oceaniadive.net.au

Payne Industries t/a Holiday Pictures
PO BOX 1294
Airlie Beach, QLD 4802
☎ 0417 388 079
email: josh@payneindustries.com

Prosail Whitsunday
PO Box 973
Airlie Beach, QLD 4802
☎ 07 4946 7533
www.prosail.com.au

Reef Safari Dive
PO Box 24
Airlie Beach, QLD 4802
☎ 07 4946 4766
www.reefsafari.com

Tallarook Sail & Dive Charters
16 Commerce Cl
Airlie Beach, QLD 4802
☎ 07 4946 4855
www.tallarookdive.com.au

HAMILTON ISLAND

H2O Sportz
PO Box 19
Hamilton Island, QLD 4803
☎ 07 4946 9888
www.h2osportz.com.au

AYR

Yongala Dive Pty Ltd
Po Box 841
Ayr, QLD 4807
☎ 07 4783 1519
www.yongaladive.com.au

TOWNSVILLE

Adrenalin Dive
PO Box 5429
Townsville, QLD 4810
☎ 07 4724 0600
www.adrenalindive.com.au

Mike Ball Dive Expeditions
143 Lake St
Townsville, QLD 4810
☎ 07 4053 0501
www.mikeball.com

Ocean Dive Australia
3 Jean St
Townsville, QLD 4819
☎ 07 4758 1391
www.oceandive.com.au

Pro Dive Townsville
PO BOX 2126
Townsville, QLD 4810
☎ 07 4721 1760
www.prodivetownsville.com.au

CAIRNS

B.C.C.S. Pty Ltd
9 Quondong Close
Cairns, QLD 4870
☎ 07 4053 3777
email: bruce_cock@bigpond.com

Big Cat Green Island Reef Cruises
The Reef Terminal, 1 Spence St
Cairns, QLD 4870
☎ 07 4051 0444
www.bigcat-cruises.com.au

Captain Cook Cruises
PO Box 4927
Cairns, QLD 4870
☎ 07 4031 4433
www.captaincook.com.au

Coral Princess Cruises
PO Box 2093
Cairns, QLD 4870
☎ 07 4040 9999
www.coralprincess.com.au

Deep Sea Divers Den
PO Box 5264
Cairns, QLD 4870
☎ 07 4046 7333
www.divers-den.com

Dive 7 Seas
153 Sheridan Street
Cairns, QLD 4870
☎ 07 4041 2700
www.dive7s.com

Dive Centre
PO Box 2401
Cairns, QLD 4870
☎ 07 4051 0294
www.cairnsdive.com

Diversion Dive Travel & Training
PO Box 191
Cairns, QLD 4870
☎ 07 4039 0200
www.diversionOZ.com

Diving Academy
PO BOX 2365
Cairns, QLD 4870
☎ 07 4031 9299
www.cairnsda.com

Explorer Ventures Australia
PO Box 6905
Cairns, QLD 4870
☎ 07 4031 5566
www.explorerventures.com

Hostel Reef Trips
100 Abbott Street
Cairns, QLD 4870
☎ 07 4031 7217
www.reeftrip.com

Il Mare Pty Ltd
Po Box 861 WA
Cairns, QLD 4870
☎ 07 4036 3581
email: info@bluekarem.com

Inn the Tropics
141 Sheridan Street
Cairns, QLD 4870
☎ 0418 783 601
www.innthetropics.com

IRES
PO Box 468
Cairns, QLD 4870
☎ 07 4081 6600
www.ires.com.au

MCL Australia
PO Box 861
Cairns, QLD 4870
☎ 0412 200 140
email: don@bluearem.com

Ocean Spirit Cruises/Dive
PO Box 2140
Cairns, QLD 4870
☎ 07 4031 2920
www.oceanspirt.com.au

PADI Asia Pacific
13 Turner St
Cairns, QLD 4870
☎ 0417 006 658
www.padi.com

Passions of Paradise
PO Box 2145
Cairns, QLD 4870
☎ 07 4041 1600
www.passions.com.au

ProDive
PO Box 5551
Cairns, QLD 4870
☎ 07 4031 5255
www.prodive-cairns.com.au

Reef Magic Cruises
PO Box 905
Cairns, QLD 4870
☎ 07 4031 1598
www.reefmagiccruises.com

Rum Runner Dive and Sail
PO Box 127
Cairns, QLD 4870
☎ 07 4098 0061
www.rumrunner.com.au

Santa Maria Yacht Cruises
PO Box 5957
Cairns, QLD 4870
☎ 07 4031 0558
www.reefcharter.com

Scuba Air
PO Box 1380
Cairns, QLD 4870
☎ 07 4035 5035
www.cairns-scuba-air.com

Scubapix
PO Box 7470
Cairns, QLD 4870
☎ 07 4031 7655
www.@scubapix.com

Seastar Cruises
PO Box 835E
Cairns, QLD 4870
☎ 07 4033 0333
www.seastarcruises.com.au

Seawalker Australia Pty Ltd
PO Box 6785
Cairns, QLD 4868
☎ 07 4045 0791
email: kvksw@yahoo.com.au

Spirit Of Freedom
PO Box 1276
Cairns, QLD 4870
☎ 07 4031 2490
www.spiritoffreedom.com.au

SSI Australia
PO Box 2454
Cairns, QLD 4870
☎ 07 4044 4999
www.ssidiving.com

S2 Dive
PO Box 1772
Cairns, QLD 4870
☎ 07 4031 3921
www.s2club.net

Sunlover Cruises
PO Box 835
Cairns, QLD 4870
☎ 07 4050 1331
www.sunlover.com.au

Taka Dive Adventures
PO Box 6592
Cairns, QLD 4870
☎ 07 4051 8722
www.takadive.com.au

The Woolshed Chargrill & Saloon Bar
PO Box 2204
Cairns, QLD 4870
☎ 07 4031 6304
www.thewoolshed.com.au

Tusa Dive Charters
PO Box 1276
Cairns, QLD 4870
☎ 07 4031 2490
www.tusadive.com

PORT DOUGLAS

Aristocat Reef Cruises
PO Box 599
Port Douglas, QLD 4871
☎ 03 9836 4466
www.aristocat.com.au

Calypso Reef Charters
PO Box 653
Port Douglas, QLD 4871
☎ 07 4099 6999
www.calypsocharters.com.au

Haba Dive
PO Box 122
Port Douglas, QLD 4871
☎ 07 4099 5254
www.habadive.com.au

Quicksilver Connections
PO Box 171
Port Douglas, QLD 4871
☎ 07 4087 2150
☎ 07 4099 5525
www.quicksilver-cruises.com

Quicksilver Dive/Sable Lake Pty Ltd
PO Box 228
Port Douglas QLD 4871
☎ 07 4099 5050
gary@quicksilverdive.com.au
www.quicksilverdive.com

Tech Dive Academy
PO Box 436
Port Douglas, QLD 4871
☎ 07 4099 6880
www.tech-dive-academy.com

Undersea Explorer
PO Box 615
Port Douglas, QLD 4871
☎ 07 4099 5911
www.undersea.com.au

Index